The Infinite Key

The Infinite Key

Matthew Petchinsky

The Infinite Key: Unlocking the Secrets to Prosperity, Resilience, and Purpose
By: Matthew Petchinsky

Introduction: Why This Book Is for Everyone

In the ever-evolving world of authorship, where trends shift rapidly and success often feels like an elusive dream, there exists a universal truth: the tools to achieve greatness are within reach of everyone. Whether you are a seasoned author with multiple bestsellers under your belt or someone taking their very first steps into the world of writing, this book was created with one simple yet powerful promise: to provide the ultimate toolset you need to succeed, regardless of your circumstances.

A Universal Guide for All Authors

No matter your starting point, this book is for you. Are you an author constrained by time, juggling your creative pursuits with a busy schedule? Do you feel limited by financial challenges, wondering how to launch your book or make it thrive without breaking the bank? Or perhaps you're overwhelmed by the complexities of marketing, self-publishing, or even finding your unique voice in a crowded literary space. Whatever your situation, this book has been designed to address your needs.

Here, you will find strategies that are adaptable to any time and place. You don't need a massive advertising budget, a team of experts, or even a perfect plan. What you do need is a willingness to learn, adapt, and implement the steps laid out for you. The pages ahead are filled with actionable advice, proven methods, and insightful wisdom, all distilled into a clear and approachable format that you can use no matter where you are in your writing journey.

The Promise: Your Success Is Non-Negotiable

This book was not created to add to the noise or offer generic advice. It was written with the conviction that every author, regardless of their background or resources, has the potential to succeed. The world of publishing is not reserved for the elite few or those with privileged connections—it belongs to anyone with the determination to make their voice heard.

Within these pages, you will discover how to:

- **Navigate any financial situation:** Learn low-cost and no-cost strategies that can propel your book into the hands of readers without straining your budget.
- **Master time management:** Discover how to carve out the time you need to write, market, and grow your author career, even with the busiest of schedules.
- **Overcome location barriers:** Whether you're in a bustling city or a remote village, you'll gain tools and techniques that transcend physical limitations, using the power of digital platforms and creative outreach.

Why This Book Matters Now More Than Ever

We live in a time of unprecedented opportunity for authors. Technology has leveled the playing field, giving everyone access to tools that once belonged only to the elite few. Yet, with this abundance of opportunity comes an overwhelming sea of choices, strategies, and opinions. It's easy to feel lost, to wonder if your efforts will ever amount to success.

This book serves as your guiding star, cutting through the noise to provide clarity, focus, and a roadmap to achieving your dreams. It doesn't matter if you're struggling to write your first draft or navigating the complexities of marketing your tenth novel—these tools are designed to meet you where you are and elevate you to where you want to be.

The Ultimate Tool: A Timeless Resource for Timeless Success

The promise of this book is simple but profound: success in authorship is not about luck, timing, or circumstance—it's about having the right tools and using them effectively. This book provides those tools, tailored to fit your unique situation and designed to empower you to take control of your author journey.

By the end of this book, you will not only have the knowledge to succeed but also the confidence to implement it. You will understand that success is not reserved for others; it is something you can achieve, starting right now, no matter where you are in life.

So turn the page, embrace the journey, and prepare to unlock the potential that has always been within you. This book is your key to a future of limitless possibilities. Success is waiting—you only need to reach for it.

Part I: The Mindset Shift

Chapter 1: The Power of Purpose
How Identifying and Refining Your Purpose Drives Sustainable Success

Success is not an accident; it is the deliberate result of clarity, determination, and sustained effort. At the core of all sustainable success lies a singular, irreplaceable force: purpose. Purpose is the engine that powers creativity, the compass that guides decision-making, and the wellspring of resilience that keeps us moving forward even when the journey becomes challenging. In this chapter, we will explore the profound impact of identifying and refining your purpose and how it can transform your author journey into a meaningful and sustainable endeavor.

What Is Purpose and Why Does It Matter?

Purpose is more than a fleeting motivation or an abstract ideal; it is the deeply personal reason behind your actions. It's what gives your work meaning and provides a sense of fulfillment that goes beyond external achievements like book sales or awards. While goals are measurable and finite, purpose is enduring. Goals may evolve, but your purpose serves as a constant foundation upon which all your efforts are built.

In the context of writing and publishing, your purpose might encompass one or more of the following:

- Sharing a story or message that needs to be told.
- Inspiring others to see the world in new ways.
- Creating art that brings joy or reflection.
- Providing practical knowledge or transformative insights.
- Building a legacy that outlives you.

Without a clear sense of purpose, even the most talented author can become lost in the hustle of deadlines, marketing strategies, and the pressure to "keep up" in a competitive market. Purpose anchors you, ensuring that your efforts are not only productive but also meaningful.

How to Identify Your Purpose

Identifying your purpose is a deeply introspective process that requires honesty, patience, and curiosity. Here are steps to uncovering the purpose that will fuel your sustainable success:

1. **Reflect on Your Why**

    Ask yourself: *Why do I want to write? What compels me to create?* Reflect on moments when writing brought you joy, healing, or clarity. Think about what drives you to sit down and commit words to the page, even when no one else is watching.

2. **Examine Your Values**

    Your purpose is often closely tied to your core values. What principles guide your life? Is it creativity, connection, truth, empowerment, or something else? Aligning your writing goals with your values ensures your work remains authentic and fulfilling.

3. **Identify Your Audience**

    Purpose often finds its fullest expression when it serves others. Who do you hope to reach with your writing? Whether your audience is niche or broad, visualizing the people you want to impact can clarify the purpose behind your work.

4. **Define Success on Your Terms**

    What does success look like to you? Is it measured by personal growth, the number of lives you touch, or financial independence? Defining success helps you understand how your purpose intersects with your goals.

5. **Write Your Purpose Statement**

    Summarize your reflections into a clear purpose statement, such as:
    - *"To inspire others through stories of resilience and triumph."*
    - *"To empower readers with knowledge that transforms their lives."*
    - *"To create worlds that spark joy and ignite imagination."*

Keep this statement where you can see it, revisiting it often to keep your efforts aligned with your purpose.

The Role of Purpose in Sustainable Success

Purpose is more than a starting point; it is the driving force behind enduring achievement. Here's how purpose fuels sustainable success:

1. **Clarity in Decision-Making**

    Purpose acts as a filter through which all decisions are made. Should you take on a particular project, collaborate with a certain individual, or invest time in a specific marketing strategy? When your purpose is clear, it becomes easier to discern which opportunities align with your vision and which are distractions.

2. **Intrinsic Motivation**

    External rewards like accolades and financial success are fleeting. Purpose, on the other hand, provides intrinsic motivation that sustains you through challenges and setbacks. When your purpose is rooted in something meaningful, even obstacles become opportunities for growth.

3. **Resilience and Persistence**

    The path to success is rarely linear. There will be moments of rejection, self-doubt, and uncertainty. A strong sense of purpose keeps you grounded and reminds you of the bigger picture, enabling you to persevere when others might give up.

4. **Connection with Readers**

    Readers are drawn to authenticity. When your work is infused with purpose, it resonates on a deeper level, forging meaningful connections that transcend the page. This connection not only builds a loyal audience but also creates a lasting impact.

Refining Your Purpose Over Time

Purpose is not static; it evolves as you grow as a person and an author. Refining your purpose involves:

- **Continuous Reflection:** Periodically revisit your purpose to ensure it still aligns with your goals and values.
- **Learning from Feedback:** Reader feedback can provide valuable insights into how your work is received and how it aligns with your intended impact.
- **Embracing Change:** Don't be afraid to pivot if your purpose shifts. Growth often brings new perspectives that can deepen your sense of direction.

Taking Action: Purpose in Practice

To harness the power of purpose, integrate it into your daily writing and professional life:

- Start each writing session by revisiting your purpose statement to remind yourself why your work matters.
- Use your purpose as a guiding principle when setting goals, making decisions, and evaluating progress.

- Share your purpose with your audience through authentic storytelling and engagement.

Conclusion: Purpose as Your North Star

In the vast and sometimes overwhelming world of writing and publishing, purpose is your North Star. It is the unshakable foundation that keeps you grounded, the beacon that guides you through uncharted waters, and the fire that fuels your creativity and ambition.

By identifying and refining your purpose, you unlock the power to create work that is not only successful but also deeply fulfilling. This is the cornerstone of sustainable success—writing with intention, living with authenticity, and achieving your dreams with clarity and conviction.

Let your purpose be the engine that drives your journey, ensuring that every step you take leads to a destination worthy of your efforts.

Chapter 2: Unshakable Confidence
Techniques to Cultivate Unwavering Self-Belief Through Any Hardship

Confidence is often viewed as an elusive quality, something that some people are born with while others must struggle to obtain. But the truth is, confidence is not a fixed trait; it is a skill—a mindset that can be developed, strengthened, and maintained over time. For authors, confidence is the fuel that powers creativity, the armor that protects against rejection, and the foundation that enables you to share your voice unapologetically with the world.

In this chapter, we will explore practical, proven techniques to cultivate unshakable confidence, equipping you to face any hardship with resilience and self-belief.

What Is Confidence and Why Is It Crucial?

Confidence is not arrogance or an inflated sense of self; it is a quiet, steady belief in your abilities and your worth. It's the conviction that you have something valuable to offer, even in the face of challenges or criticism. For writers, confidence manifests in several key ways:

- The courage to start a project without second-guessing your talent.
- The persistence to keep going when faced with rejection or creative blocks.
- The willingness to share your work with the world, knowing it won't resonate with everyone—but it will resonate with the right audience.

Without confidence, even the most talented author may hesitate, procrastinate, or give up altogether. Confidence is not only crucial for creating but also for navigating the highs and lows of the writing journey.

The Relationship Between Confidence and Hardship

Confidence does not mean an absence of fear, doubt, or hardship. Instead, it is the ability to move forward despite those challenges. Hardship is an inevitable part of any creative endeavor. Writers face rejection, harsh criticism, slow sales, and the constant demand to innovate. Yet, it is through these hardships that confidence can grow the strongest.

The key is to view hardship not as a threat to your confidence but as an opportunity to strengthen it. Each challenge you face and overcome adds another layer to your self-belief, proving to yourself that you are capable of enduring and thriving.

Techniques to Cultivate Unshakable Confidence

1. Reframe Negative Self-Talk

The way you speak to yourself shapes your confidence. Negative self-talk—statements like "I'm not good enough," "I'll never finish this book," or "Nobody will want to read this"—undermines your belief in your abilities.

Action Steps:

- **Identify the Inner Critic:** Pay attention to the negative thoughts that arise when you face challenges. Write them down to become more aware of them.
- **Challenge the Narrative:** Ask yourself if these thoughts are rooted in fact or fear. Often, they are baseless assumptions.
- **Replace with Affirmations:** Develop positive affirmations that align with your goals, such as "I am a capable and talented writer" or "My words have value and impact." Repeat these daily.

2. Focus on Progress, Not Perfection

Perfectionism is one of the greatest threats to confidence. When you set unattainable standards, every perceived failure feels like a confirmation of inadequacy. Instead, shift your focus to progress.

Action Steps:

- Celebrate small wins, such as finishing a draft, brainstorming a new idea, or receiving positive feedback.
- Break larger goals into manageable steps to create a sense of achievement with each milestone.
- Remind yourself that every great author started where you are now—with imperfect drafts and countless revisions.

3. Build a Resilient Mindset

Resilience is the ability to bounce back from setbacks, and it is closely tied to confidence. Developing resilience ensures that challenges don't erode your self-belief but instead become stepping stones to growth.

Action Steps:

- **Adopt a Growth Mindset:** View mistakes and failures as opportunities to learn and improve rather than as reflections of your worth.
- **Seek Feedback Wisely:** Constructive feedback is invaluable, but not all opinions are created equal. Learn to differentiate between helpful critique and unproductive negativity.
- **Practice Gratitude:** Focus on what's going well in your journey. Gratitude can shift your mindset from scarcity to abundance, reinforcing your belief in your potential.

4. Visualize Success

Visualization is a powerful tool for building confidence. When you vividly imagine yourself succeeding, you activate the same neural pathways as if you were experiencing success in real life. This trains your brain to expect and believe in positive outcomes.

Action Steps:

- Set aside time each day to visualize yourself achieving your writing goals. Picture your book being published, receiving praise, or inspiring readers.
- Engage all your senses in the visualization process to make it more impactful. Imagine the joy of holding your book, the sound of applause, or the words of a heartfelt review.

5. Surround Yourself with Positivity

Your environment significantly impacts your confidence. The people you interact with, the content you consume, and even the physical spaces where you work can either build or diminish your self-belief.

Action Steps:

- Connect with supportive communities of writers who understand and encourage your journey.
- Seek mentors or role models who inspire confidence through their own success stories.
- Create a workspace that uplifts you, with affirming reminders of your goals and achievements.

6. Take Action Despite Fear

Confidence grows through action. The more you step outside your comfort zone and take risks, the more you prove to yourself that you are capable.

Action Steps:

- Identify one fear that's holding you back—whether it's submitting your manuscript, sharing your work publicly, or trying a new genre.
- Take one small, manageable step toward facing that fear. For example, share a chapter with a trusted friend or submit to a low-stakes contest.
- Celebrate the courage it took to act, regardless of the outcome.

7. Develop a Daily Confidence Routine

Confidence is like a muscle—it strengthens with consistent effort. Developing a daily routine to nurture your self-belief ensures it remains strong even during difficult times.

Action Steps:

- Start your day with affirmations or journaling about your strengths and accomplishments.
- Dedicate time each day to activities that build confidence, such as writing, learning, or seeking inspiration.
- End your day by reflecting on what went well and what you're proud of.

The Ripple Effect of Confidence

When you cultivate unshakable confidence, its benefits extend beyond your writing. Confidence affects how you approach opportunities, connect with others, and handle challenges. It also creates a ripple effect, inspiring others to believe in themselves and their work.

Readers are drawn to confident authors who trust their voice and vision. Confidence allows you to market your work authentically, collaborate effectively, and embrace the challenges of authorship with grace.

Conclusion: Becoming Your Own Advocate

Unshakable confidence is not about erasing fear or hardship; it's about trusting yourself to navigate through them. It's about becoming your own advocate—believing in your ability to succeed, even when the odds seem stacked against you.

By reframing negative self-talk, focusing on progress, and taking deliberate actions to build resilience, you can cultivate a self-belief that no external force can shake. Let confidence become the foundation of your journey, empowering you to face challenges head-on and emerge stronger, wiser, and more determined than ever.

Chapter 3: Mastering Adaptability

How to Pivot and Thrive in Rapidly Changing Environments, From Technology to Life Circumstances

Adaptability is a critical skill for success in any field, but for authors, it is nothing short of essential. The publishing world is in a constant state of flux, with new technologies, trends, and reader expectations reshaping the landscape. Beyond the professional realm, personal challenges—financial setbacks, time constraints, or unforeseen life events—can test an author's ability to remain productive and focused.

Mastering adaptability is about more than surviving these changes; it's about using them as opportunities to grow, innovate, and thrive. In this chapter, we'll explore how adaptability empowers authors to navigate change with confidence, pivot when necessary, and find success in the most unexpected circumstances.

The Necessity of Adaptability

In a world that is constantly evolving, those who resist change risk stagnation, while those who embrace it flourish. Adaptability is the ability to adjust to new conditions, whether they are anticipated or come as a surprise. It allows you to:

- Stay relevant in a rapidly changing market.
- Overcome obstacles and challenges with resilience.
- Recognize and seize new opportunities as they arise.
- Maintain productivity and creativity in the face of uncertainty.

For authors, this means being open to learning new tools, exploring unconventional strategies, and adjusting your plans as circumstances change. Adaptability isn't about abandoning your vision; it's about finding new ways to achieve it.

Common Challenges That Require Adaptability

1. Technological Advances

From self-publishing platforms to AI-driven editing tools and marketing algorithms, technology is reshaping the way authors create, publish, and promote their work. Staying ahead requires a willingness to embrace these tools rather than fear them.

2. Shifting Reader Preferences

Trends in genres, formats, and storytelling styles can change quickly. What was popular yesterday might lose traction tomorrow. Authors who are in tune with their audience and willing to adapt their approach can thrive in any trend cycle.

3. Life Circumstances

Unexpected events like health challenges, family obligations, or financial pressures can disrupt even the most carefully laid plans. Adaptability ensures you can pivot without losing sight of your goals.

4. Market Saturation and Competition

The ease of self-publishing has led to a flood of new books on the market, making it harder to stand out. Adaptable authors find creative ways to differentiate themselves and connect with readers.

Techniques to Master Adaptability
1. Cultivate a Growth Mindset

A growth mindset is the belief that abilities and intelligence can be developed through effort and learning. This mindset is the cornerstone of adaptability, as it fosters resilience and a willingness to embrace change.

Action Steps:

- Replace fixed beliefs like "I'm not good with technology" with "I can learn to use new tools effectively."
- View challenges as opportunities to grow rather than as insurmountable obstacles.
- Celebrate progress and learning, no matter how small.

2. Embrace Lifelong Learning

The most adaptable authors are those who continuously invest in their education. Whether it's mastering new technologies, staying current on industry trends, or developing new writing techniques, ongoing learning keeps you prepared for change.

Action Steps:

- Dedicate time each week to learning something new, whether through online courses, books, or webinars.
- Follow industry leaders, attend writing conferences, or join communities where trends and tools are discussed.
- Experiment with emerging technologies, such as AI writing assistants or social media marketing platforms, to see how they can enhance your process.

3. Develop Flexibility in Goal Setting

Adaptable authors understand the importance of setting goals but also recognize when those goals need to be adjusted. Flexibility allows you to respond to new opportunities or challenges without feeling like you've failed.

Action Steps:

- Break goals into smaller, adaptable steps that can be adjusted as needed.
- Regularly review your goals to ensure they remain relevant and achievable in light of changing circumstances.
- Focus on outcomes rather than rigid methods. For example, if your goal is to reach readers, explore multiple formats like audiobooks, eBooks, or serialized content.

4. Build a Resilient Routine

While adaptability requires flexibility, it's important to establish routines that anchor you during times of change. A resilient routine includes habits that keep you grounded and productive, even when everything else feels uncertain.

Action Steps:

- Identify core habits that support your writing, such as daily word counts, regular brainstorming sessions, or dedicated marketing time.
- Prioritize routines that are easy to adjust. For example, if your morning writing session is disrupted, find time later in the day to make up for it.
- Use tools like planners or productivity apps to stay organized, even during chaotic periods.

5. Stay Attuned to Reader Needs

Understanding your audience is key to thriving in a shifting market. Adaptable authors regularly engage with their readers to stay informed about preferences, trends, and expectations.

Action Steps:

- Interact with readers through social media, newsletters, or virtual events to gather feedback and insights.
- Analyze sales data and reviews to identify what resonates with your audience and what doesn't.
- Experiment with different genres, styles, or formats to meet evolving reader preferences.

6. Build a Strong Network

Connections with other authors, editors, marketers, and industry professionals can provide valuable support and guidance during times of change. A strong network can help you navigate challenges and discover new opportunities.

Action Steps:

- Join writing communities, online forums, or professional organizations.
- Collaborate with others on projects or promotions to expand your reach and learn from their experiences.
- Seek out mentors or peers who can offer advice and encouragement when you need to pivot.

7. Practice Mindfulness and Emotional Resilience

Adaptability requires not only practical skills but also emotional resilience. Change can be stressful, and the ability to stay calm and focused is crucial.

Action Steps:

- Incorporate mindfulness practices like meditation or journaling into your routine to manage stress.

- Reframe setbacks as temporary and focus on the bigger picture.
- Surround yourself with supportive people who uplift and encourage you.

Adapting to Real-World Challenges

Scenario 1: Embracing Self-Publishing Technology

Imagine the traditional publishing route you've been pursuing becomes inaccessible. Rather than giving up, you learn to navigate self-publishing platforms like Amazon Kindle Direct Publishing (KDP) or IngramSpark, using tutorials and peer support to master the process.

Scenario 2: Pivoting in a Changing Market

You've spent months writing a book in a genre that suddenly declines in popularity. Instead of shelving the project, you reframe the story to align with a more current trend or market it to a niche audience that still values the genre.

Scenario 3: Balancing Life Circumstances

A family emergency disrupts your writing schedule. Rather than abandoning your goals, you adapt by writing in shorter bursts or focusing on promotional activities until you can return to a full schedule.

Conclusion: Thriving Through Change

Mastering adaptability is not just about weathering the storm; it's about finding ways to thrive in the rain. By cultivating a growth mindset, staying flexible, and embracing change as an opportunity for growth, you can turn challenges into stepping stones for success.

Adaptability ensures that no matter what the world throws your way—be it a new technology, shifting trends, or unexpected life events—you can pivot with confidence and purpose. The ability to adjust and thrive is not just a skill; it's a superpower that will set you apart as an author ready to navigate any landscape.

Chapter 4: Abundance Mindset in a Scarcity World

Understanding Abundance and Creating Wealth Opportunities in All Situations

In a world where scarcity is often emphasized—limited resources, economic downturns, and fierce competition—it is easy to feel trapped by the belief that opportunities are few and far between. This scarcity mindset fosters fear, insecurity, and self-doubt, making it difficult to see beyond immediate challenges. But there is an alternative: an abundance mindset.

An abundance mindset shifts your perspective from lack to possibility, enabling you to recognize and create wealth opportunities even in the most challenging circumstances. This chapter delves into the principles of an abundance mindset, offering actionable strategies to cultivate this transformative perspective and use it to generate success and wealth in any situation.

What Is an Abundance Mindset?

An abundance mindset is the belief that opportunities, resources, and success are plentiful. It rejects the idea that life is a zero-sum game where someone else's gain is your loss. Instead, it embraces the idea that success is expandable and that there is enough for everyone to thrive.

For authors, this means understanding that:

- There are countless readers in the world, and your unique voice will resonate with the right audience.
- Success is not about competing with other writers but about finding your niche and delivering value.
- Financial rewards are not limited to traditional publishing; wealth can be created through innovative approaches like self-publishing, digital content, and diversified income streams.

An abundance mindset empowers you to focus on possibilities rather than limitations, unlocking creativity, resilience, and a proactive approach to challenges.

The Scarcity Mindset vs. the Abundance Mindset
Characteristics of a Scarcity Mindset

- Fear of failure or rejection.
- Obsessing over competition and comparing yourself to others.
- Viewing setbacks as insurmountable.
- Believing opportunities are few and fleeting.

Characteristics of an Abundance Mindset

- Confidence that opportunities are always available.
- Focusing on collaboration and mutual growth rather than competition.
- Viewing challenges as stepping stones to success.
- Believing in the value of your work and your ability to create wealth.

The Science Behind an Abundance Mindset

Psychological studies reveal that mindset shapes behavior and outcomes. A scarcity mindset activates stress responses, narrowing focus and limiting problem-solving abilities. In contrast, an abundance mindset fosters optimism, creativity, and strategic thinking, enabling you to identify and act on opportunities that others might overlook.

By shifting to an abundance mindset, you train your brain to look for solutions rather than dwelling on problems. This change not only improves your mental well-being but also enhances your ability to generate wealth and success.

Techniques to Cultivate an Abundance Mindset

1. Reframe Negative Thoughts

Scarcity thinking often manifests as self-defeating thoughts like "I'll never make enough money" or "There are too many authors already." Reframing these thoughts is essential.

Action Steps:

- Replace "I'll never make enough money" with "I am actively creating multiple income streams."
- Replace "There are too many authors already" with "My unique voice will resonate with the right audience."
- Practice gratitude daily to shift focus from what you lack to what you have.

2. Recognize and Expand Your Value

Understanding and embracing your unique strengths is key to creating wealth opportunities. Your value as an author goes beyond your writing; it includes your knowledge, perspective, and ability to connect with readers.

Action Steps:

- Identify your strengths, such as storytelling, research skills, or marketing abilities.
- Explore ways to monetize these strengths, such as offering writing workshops, creating digital guides, or freelance writing.
- Continuously refine your skills to increase your value.

3. Diversify Your Income Streams

An abundance mindset recognizes that wealth is not limited to one source. Authors can create financial stability by diversifying income streams.

Action Steps:

- Expand beyond book sales by offering related products or services, such as merchandise, courses, or consulting.
- Consider different publishing formats, such as audiobooks, serialized content, or eBooks.
- Explore passive income opportunities, such as affiliate marketing or royalties from self-published works.

4. Build Collaborative Relationships

Collaboration, not competition, is the hallmark of an abundance mindset. Partnering with others creates opportunities for mutual growth and success.

Action Steps:

- Connect with other authors for joint promotions, anthologies, or co-writing projects.
- Engage with your readers to build a loyal community that supports your work.
- Network with industry professionals who can open doors to new opportunities.

5. Focus on Long-Term Growth

A scarcity mindset is often preoccupied with immediate results, while an abundance mindset prioritizes sustainable growth. Building wealth takes time and consistency.

Action Steps:

- Invest in your author brand through a professional website, social media presence, and engaging content.
- Develop a long-term plan for writing, publishing, and marketing that aligns with your goals.
- Celebrate progress, even if it feels incremental, and trust in the process of growth.

Creating Wealth Opportunities in Any Situation

1. Leveraging Technology

Technology provides countless tools for authors to create wealth, from self-publishing platforms to social media marketing. Embracing these tools expands your reach and potential earnings.

Examples:

- Use Amazon KDP, IngramSpark, or other platforms to self-publish and retain higher royalties.
- Market your books through targeted ads, email campaigns, or social media.
- Create digital products, such as downloadable guides or eCourses, to generate passive income.

2. Turning Challenges into Opportunities

Every challenge contains the seeds of opportunity. The key is to approach difficulties with curiosity and creativity.

Examples:

- If sales are slow, focus on building your audience through free content like blogs or podcasts.
- If you face a financial setback, explore crowdfunding options to fund your next project.
- If you encounter writer's block, use the time to learn new skills or explore alternative genres.

3. Tapping Into Underserved Markets

An abundance mindset encourages you to look for opportunities where others might not. Niche markets often have less competition and more dedicated audiences.

Examples:

- Write books tailored to specific communities or interests, such as niche hobbies or underserved demographics.
- Offer translations of your work to reach international audiences.
- Create content for emerging trends, such as short reads for busy professionals or AI-generated audiobooks.

The Ripple Effect of Abundance

An abundance mindset not only benefits you but also positively impacts those around you. By sharing your knowledge, collaborating with others, and contributing to your community, you create a ripple effect of abundance. Success multiplies when shared.

For example:

- Offering free resources or advice to aspiring authors can build goodwill and expand your audience.
- Supporting other authors' work fosters a culture of collaboration and mutual success.
- Investing in your readers through engagement and exclusive content strengthens their loyalty and support.

Conclusion: Creating Wealth Through Abundance

The journey to success and wealth begins in the mind. By cultivating an abundance mindset, you unlock the ability to see opportunities where others see obstacles, to innovate where others stagnate, and to thrive where others struggle.

Wealth is not just about money; it's about creating value, building connections, and leaving a lasting impact. With the principles and techniques outlined in this chapter, you can transform scarcity into possibility and build a future where success is not only achievable but abundant.

Chapter 5: Mental Resilience
Exercises and Practices for Building Mental Toughness That Authors Can Apply Daily

Writing is a deeply personal and often solitary endeavor. Authors pour their hearts into their work, making them vulnerable to criticism, self-doubt, and external challenges. Mental resilience—the ability to persevere, adapt, and thrive in the face of adversity—is an essential skill for any author striving for success.

In this chapter, we'll explore the concept of mental resilience and provide actionable exercises and practices that authors can incorporate into their daily routines to build mental toughness and maintain focus, determination, and creativity.

What Is Mental Resilience?

Mental resilience is the capacity to handle stress, setbacks, and uncertainty without losing momentum or succumbing to self-doubt. It is not about avoiding challenges but rather about learning to navigate them with grace and determination. For authors, mental resilience involves:

- Staying motivated despite rejection or criticism.
- Overcoming creative blocks and maintaining productivity.
- Remaining focused on long-term goals amidst distractions or life challenges.
- Cultivating a positive mindset that fuels creativity and innovation.

The Importance of Mental Resilience for Authors

1. Rejection Is Part of the Journey

Rejection is inevitable in the writing world, whether it's from publishers, agents, or readers. Mental resilience helps authors view rejection as a stepping stone rather than a roadblock.

2. Writing Requires Patience and Persistence

Completing a manuscript, revising drafts, and navigating the publishing process take time. Resilience ensures that authors stay committed and motivated throughout these long and often unpredictable phases.

3. Creativity Is Not Always Linear

Authors face creative blocks, self-doubt, and moments of burnout. Mental toughness enables them to push through these periods and rediscover their creative spark.

Daily Exercises and Practices for Building Mental Resilience

1. Start with Mindful Morning Routines

How you begin your day sets the tone for everything that follows. A mindful morning routine helps cultivate clarity, focus, and positivity.

Practice:

- **Gratitude Journaling:** Spend 5 minutes listing things you're grateful for, such as your writing progress, supportive friends, or opportunities to create.
- **Affirmations:** Repeat positive statements like "I am capable of achieving my goals" or "My creativity flows effortlessly."
- **Mindful Breathing:** Take 5 deep breaths, focusing on the inhale and exhale, to ground yourself before starting the day.

2. Set Small, Achievable Goals

Large goals can feel overwhelming, especially when progress seems slow. Breaking them down into smaller tasks makes them more manageable and provides regular opportunities to celebrate achievements.

Practice:

- Use the SMART (Specific, Measurable, Achievable, Relevant, Time-bound) method to set daily writing goals.
- For example: "Write 500 words today" or "Edit one chapter by noon."
- Celebrate each milestone, no matter how small, to reinforce a sense of accomplishment.

3. Reframe Negative Thoughts

Negative self-talk is a common challenge for authors, often triggered by rejection, criticism, or comparison to others. Reframing these thoughts builds mental resilience.

Practice:

- Identify recurring negative thoughts, such as "I'm not good enough" or "I'll never succeed."
- Challenge their validity by asking, "What evidence supports this thought?" or "What would I say to a friend in this situation?"
- Replace negative thoughts with empowering ones: "Every writer faces challenges, and I am learning and growing through mine."

4. Develop Emotional Detachment from Feedback

While feedback is valuable for growth, it can also feel personal and overwhelming. Learning to view feedback objectively strengthens resilience.

Practice:

- When receiving feedback, focus on actionable insights rather than emotional reactions.
- Separate yourself from your work; remember, criticism of your writing is not a critique of your worth.
- Thank those who offer constructive feedback and use it as a tool for improvement.

5. Practice Visualization

Visualization helps authors build confidence and resilience by mentally rehearsing success.

Practice:

- Close your eyes and imagine yourself achieving your goals: completing your manuscript, receiving positive reviews, or holding your published book.
- Engage all your senses. Picture the colors of your book cover, feel the weight of the book in your hands, or hear the applause of an audience at a reading.
- Spend 5 minutes daily visualizing success to strengthen your belief in your abilities.

6. Embrace the Power of Breaks

Overworking leads to burnout, which undermines mental resilience. Strategic breaks enhance focus and emotional stability.

Practice:

- Use the Pomodoro Technique: Work for 25 minutes, then take a 5-minute break. After four cycles, take a longer 15–30-minute break.
- During breaks, step away from screens. Stretch, take a walk, or engage in a relaxing activity.
- View breaks as essential for replenishing energy rather than as wasted time.

7. Build a Supportive Network

A strong support system bolsters resilience by providing encouragement, advice, and camaraderie.

Practice:

- Join writing communities or critique groups where you can share experiences and receive constructive feedback.
- Connect with friends, family, or mentors who understand and support your writing goals.

- Avoid isolating yourself during difficult times; reach out for help or perspective when needed.

8. Engage in Regular Physical Activity

Physical health and mental resilience are deeply connected. Exercise reduces stress, improves focus, and boosts mood.

Practice:

- Dedicate 20–30 minutes daily to physical activity, whether it's walking, yoga, or a full workout.
- Combine movement with inspiration: listen to audiobooks, podcasts, or music that motivates you while exercising.
- Use exercise as a mental reset during periods of stress or creative block.

9. Reflect and Adapt

Resilient authors learn from their experiences and adjust their strategies accordingly. Regular reflection helps identify what's working and what needs to change.

Practice:

- At the end of each day, spend 5–10 minutes journaling about your progress, challenges, and lessons learned.
- Ask yourself: "What went well today? What can I improve tomorrow?"
- Use your reflections to refine your approach and maintain momentum.

10. Develop a Long-Term Vision

Focusing on your ultimate goals helps you stay motivated and resilient, even when facing short-term challenges.

Practice:

- Write a vision statement describing where you want to be as an author in 5–10 years.
- Revisit this vision regularly to remind yourself of the bigger picture.
- Align your daily actions with your long-term aspirations, keeping your purpose front and center.

Resilience in Action: Overcoming Common Challenges

Scenario 1: Facing Rejection

Instead of internalizing rejection, view it as part of the process. Remind yourself that every successful author has faced rejection. Reflect on the feedback (if provided) and use it to strengthen your work.

Scenario 2: Battling Creative Block

Use techniques like freewriting, brainstorming, or changing your environment to reignite creativity. Remember that blocks are temporary and can be overcome with persistence and patience.

Scenario 3: Coping with Criticism

Separate constructive criticism from personal attacks. Focus on feedback that helps you grow and ignore negativity that isn't actionable or productive.

The Long-Term Benefits of Mental Resilience

Building mental resilience is not just about surviving tough times; it's about thriving through them. Over time, resilience leads to:

- Greater confidence in your abilities.
- Increased productivity and creativity.
- A stronger connection to your purpose and goals.
- The ability to turn setbacks into opportunities for growth.

Conclusion: Strength Through Practice

Mental resilience is not a trait you're born with—it's a skill you cultivate through consistent practice. By incorporating the exercises and strategies outlined in this chapter, you can build the mental toughness needed to navigate the challenges of the writing journey and emerge stronger, wiser, and more determined than ever.

Part II: The Creativity Formula

Chapter 6: The 24-Hour Creative Spark
A Proven Method for Reigniting Creativity, Anytime and Anywhere

Creativity is the lifeblood of any author, but it doesn't always flow freely. Even the most prolific writers experience moments of creative stagnation, where ideas seem elusive, and inspiration feels out of reach. These moments can be frustrating, but they're also a natural part of the creative process. The key is learning how to reignite your creativity quickly and effectively.

This chapter introduces a proven, step-by-step method for reclaiming your creative spark within 24 hours, no matter where you are or what challenges you're facing. By embracing these techniques, you'll not only overcome creative blocks but also establish a reliable framework to access inspiration anytime you need it.

Why Creativity Fades and How to Rekindle It

Creativity ebbs and flows for a variety of reasons, including:

- Mental fatigue from overwork or stress.
- Self-doubt or perfectionism that stifles expression.
- Lack of stimulation from new ideas or experiences.
- Physical exhaustion or neglect of self-care.

Understanding the causes of creative block is the first step toward overcoming it. The 24-hour Creative Spark method addresses these root causes, revitalizing your mind, body, and imagination to reignite your creative energy.

The 24-Hour Creative Spark Method

Phase 1: Morning Reset – Clear the Mental Clutter

Morning is the ideal time to set the stage for creativity. Begin your day with activities that cleanse your mind of stress and open the door to fresh ideas.

Steps:

1. **Mindful Awakening**
   - Before reaching for your phone or diving into tasks, spend 5–10 minutes practicing mindfulness or meditation. Focus on your breath or repeat an affirmation like, *"Today is a day for creativity and inspiration."*
2. **Journaling for Clarity**
   - Write freely in a journal for 10–15 minutes. Use prompts like:
     - *What am I curious about today?*
     - *What's the story I want to tell?*
     - *What's been on my mind lately?*
   - This exercise clears mental clutter and surfaces ideas that might have been buried.
3. **Physical Activation**
   - Engage in light physical activity, such as stretching, yoga, or a brisk walk. Movement increases blood flow to the brain, boosting focus and creativity.

Phase 2: Midday Stimulation – Fuel Your Imagination

By midday, it's time to actively seek inspiration from the world around you. Creativity thrives on curiosity and exposure to new stimuli.

Steps:

1. **Engage with Art or Media**
    - Spend 30 minutes exploring creative works unrelated to your current project. Read a chapter of a novel, watch a short film, listen to music, or view visual art.
    - Pay attention to what sparks your curiosity. Note colors, themes, or emotions that resonate with you.
2. **Try a Creative Exercise**
    - Use a quick, fun exercise to stimulate your imagination. Examples include:
        - **Word Association:** Write a random word, then jot down the first 10 things it makes you think of.
        - **Story Starters:** Begin a story with a phrase like *"It all began when..."* and write for 10 minutes.
        - **Visual Prompts:** Look at a photograph or painting and imagine the story behind it.
3. **Switch Environments**
    - Creativity often blooms in new surroundings. Take your notebook or laptop to a park, café, library, or even a different room in your house.

Phase 3: Afternoon Recharge – Nourish Your Body and Mind

Creativity requires energy, so take the afternoon to recharge both physically and mentally.

Steps:

1. **Eat a Balanced Meal or Snack**
    - Opt for brain-boosting foods like nuts, berries, or dark chocolate. Stay hydrated, as even mild dehydration can impair focus and creativity.
2. **Take a Power Nap**
    - A 15–20 minute nap can refresh your mind and improve cognitive function. Use this time to let your subconscious process ideas.
3. **Disconnect to Reconnect**
    - Step away from screens and allow yourself to daydream. Daydreaming activates the brain's default mode network, a key area for creative thinking.

Phase 4: Evening Creation – Harness Your Inspiration

As the day winds down, channel the inspiration and energy you've cultivated into a focused creative session.

Steps:

1. **Set a Clear Intention**
    - Define your goal for the session. For example: *"I will write 500 words"* or *"I will sketch out a new plot outline."*
2. **Eliminate Distractions**
    - Turn off notifications, set a timer, and create a space free from interruptions.
3. **Use the Pomodoro Technique**
    - Work in focused bursts of 25 minutes, followed by 5-minute breaks. This method maintains productivity without overwhelming your mind.
4. **Embrace Imperfection**
    - Focus on getting words or ideas onto the page without worrying about perfection. Creativity flows best when you silence your inner critic.

Phase 5: Nighttime Reflection – Anchor Your Progress

End the day with reflection and gratitude, solidifying the gains you've made and preparing your mind for more creativity.

Steps:

1. **Review Your Accomplishments**
    - Write down what you achieved during the day, no matter how small. Celebrate progress, such as drafting a scene or generating new ideas.
2. **Gratitude Practice**
    - Reflect on three things you're grateful for, focusing on creative breakthroughs or moments of inspiration.
3. **Set Tomorrow's Intention**
    - Plan one creative task for the next day. This keeps your momentum going and primes your mind for continued creativity.

Additional Techniques to Enhance the 24-Hour Spark
Incorporate Play
Playfulness reduces stress and opens the mind to unexpected ideas. Try doodling, building something with your hands, or engaging in a playful activity that brings joy.
Collaborate or Share Ideas
Talking with a friend, fellow writer, or community can provide fresh perspectives and encouragement.
Practice Sensory Immersion
Use your senses to inspire creativity. Light a scented candle, listen to ambient sounds, or explore textures and colors that stimulate your imagination.
The Science Behind Creativity on Demand
Neuroscience shows that creativity is not a mysterious force but a process that can be nurtured. The brain's default mode network is activated during rest and daydreaming, while active problem-solving engages the prefrontal cortex. The 24-hour Creative Spark method leverages these principles by balancing stimulation with rest, focused work with play.
Real-World Applications
Scenario 1: Overcoming Writer's Block
You're stuck on a scene. Using the 24-hour Creative Spark method, you engage with a short film in the morning, take a walk in the afternoon, and write freely at night. By the end of the day, you've generated ideas to move forward.
Scenario 2: Finding Inspiration for a New Project
Unsure of what to write next, you try word association in the morning, explore a museum exhibit virtually during lunch, and sketch out three potential story ideas in the evening. One stands out, and you're ready to begin.
Conclusion: Creativity at Your Fingertips
The 24-hour Creative Spark method proves that creativity is not a rare gift but a skill that can be cultivated and accessed on demand. By following this structured approach, you can reignite your creative energy anytime, anywhere, turning even the most uninspired days into opportunities for growth and innovation.

Chapter 7: Breaking Writer's Block

Strategies to Overcome and Eliminate Writer's Block for Good

Writer's block is the nemesis of creativity, a frustrating and often paralyzing experience that every author encounters at some point. Whether it manifests as a temporary inability to find the right words or a prolonged period of creative drought, writer's block can feel insurmountable. However, it is neither permanent nor inevitable. With the right strategies, you can overcome and eliminate writer's block, turning it from a source of frustration into an opportunity for growth.

This chapter provides a comprehensive toolkit of techniques and strategies to help you break through writer's block, build momentum, and regain your creative confidence.

Understanding Writer's Block

Writer's block is not a singular problem but a symptom of deeper issues. To overcome it, you must first identify its underlying cause. Common reasons for writer's block include:

1. Perfectionism

The fear of not being "good enough" can prevent you from starting or finishing your work.

2. Lack of Inspiration

Sometimes, your creative well runs dry, leaving you unsure of what to write or where to take your story.

3. Burnout

Overwork and fatigue can sap your energy and enthusiasm, making it difficult to focus.

4. Self-Doubt

Negative thoughts about your abilities or the value of your work can create a mental barrier to writing.

5. Unclear Direction

A lack of clarity about your story, characters, or goals can leave you feeling stuck.

Understanding which of these factors is contributing to your block is the first step in overcoming it.

Proven Strategies to Break Writer's Block

1. Freewriting to Unlock Creativity

Freewriting is a powerful technique for bypassing your inner critic and reigniting your creative flow.

How to Do It:

- Set a timer for 10–15 minutes.
- Write whatever comes to mind, without worrying about grammar, structure, or coherence.
- If you're stuck, write "I don't know what to write" until a new thought emerges.

Why It Works:

Freewriting silences perfectionism and allows your subconscious mind to take the lead, often uncovering hidden ideas or solutions.

2. Change Your Environment

A change of scenery can refresh your perspective and stimulate creativity.

Action Steps:

- Write in a new location, such as a park, café, or library.
- Rearrange your workspace to make it more inviting and inspiring.
- Use sensory elements like music, lighting, or scents to create a new atmosphere.

Why It Works:

A new environment can disrupt routine thinking patterns and provide fresh stimuli for your imagination.

3. Set Micro-Goals

Large writing goals can feel overwhelming, especially during a creative slump. Breaking them into smaller tasks makes progress more achievable.

Action Steps:

- Instead of aiming to write a chapter, set a goal to write one paragraph or describe a single character.
- Use the Pomodoro Technique to work in focused 25-minute intervals with short breaks.
- Celebrate each small win to build momentum.

Why It Works:

Micro-goals reduce pressure and create a sense of accomplishment, motivating you to keep going.

4. Explore Writing Prompts

Writing prompts can serve as a creative jumpstart, offering a structured way to generate ideas.

Action Steps:

- Use prompts like "Write about a character who discovers a secret that changes their life" or "Describe a scene where two strangers meet under unusual circumstances."
- Adapt prompts to fit your current project or use them to experiment with new ideas.

Why It Works:

Prompts provide a starting point, reducing the intimidation of a blank page and sparking your imagination.

5. Embrace Imperfection

Perfectionism often leads to paralysis. Accepting that your first draft doesn't have to be perfect frees you to write without fear.

Action Steps:

- Give yourself permission to write a "bad" draft. Focus on getting ideas down rather than perfecting them.
- Use a mantra like "Done is better than perfect" to remind yourself that progress matters more than precision.
- Schedule editing for a separate session, so you don't interrupt your creative flow.

Why It Works:

By shifting your focus from quality to quantity, you remove the pressure that contributes to writer's block.

6. Revisit Your Why

Sometimes writer's block arises when you lose sight of your purpose or passion for a project.

Action Steps:

- Reflect on why you started writing your story. What excites you about it?
- Revisit your outline or character notes to reconnect with your original vision.
- If your project no longer inspires you, consider pivoting to a new idea that feels more meaningful.

Why It Works:

Reconnecting with your "why" reignites your motivation and provides clarity about the direction of your work.

7. Engage in Creative Cross-Training

Exploring other creative outlets can stimulate your imagination and break through mental blocks.

Action Steps:

- Try a different creative activity, such as painting, photography, or music.
- Watch films, read books, or attend performances in genres outside your usual preferences.
- Use what you learn from these experiences to enrich your writing.

Why It Works:

Creative cross-training broadens your perspective and introduces new ideas that can fuel your writing.

8. Write Out of Order

If you're stuck on a specific part of your story, skip it and work on another section that excites you.

Action Steps:

- Identify a scene, character, or dialogue that feels easier or more enjoyable to write.
- Use placeholders like "[Describe setting here]" for sections you plan to revisit later.
- Piece together your story like a puzzle, focusing on what flows naturally.

Why It Works:

Writing out of order allows you to maintain momentum while giving your subconscious time to solve the problem areas.

9. Seek External Accountability

Sharing your goals with others can create a sense of accountability that motivates you to keep writing.

Action Steps:

- Join a writing group or partner with a critique buddy.
- Participate in challenges like NaNoWriMo (National Novel Writing Month).
- Share your progress with friends, family, or social media followers.

Why It Works:

External accountability provides encouragement and structure, helping you stay committed to your goals.

10. Practice Self-Care

Physical and mental well-being are essential for sustained creativity. Neglecting self-care can exacerbate writer's block.

Action Steps:

- Prioritize sleep, nutrition, and regular exercise to maintain energy levels.
- Take breaks when needed, allowing yourself time to recharge.
- Use stress-reducing techniques like meditation or deep breathing to stay calm and focused.

Why It Works:

A healthy mind and body create the optimal conditions for creativity and problem-solving.

Eliminating Writer's Block for Good

While these strategies can help you overcome immediate blocks, building long-term resilience against writer's block requires proactive habits:

1. **Establish a Consistent Writing Routine**
   - Write at the same time each day to build discipline and reduce procrastination.
2. **Set Realistic Expectations**
   - Understand that every writer experiences ups and downs. Allow yourself grace during challenging periods.
3. **Continuously Refuel Your Creativity**
   - Regularly engage with new ideas, experiences, and learning opportunities to keep your creative well full.
4. **Develop Emotional Resilience**
   - Learn to navigate rejection, criticism, and self-doubt without letting them derail your progress.

Conclusion: Your Toolkit for Overcoming Writer's Block

Writer's block is not an insurmountable obstacle—it's a challenge that every writer can overcome with the right mindset and strategies. By understanding the root causes of your block and applying the techniques outlined in this chapter, you can not only break through creative slumps but also build the confidence and resilience needed to face future challenges.

Chapter 8: Creativity on Demand

How to Tap Into Endless Inspiration, Regardless of Your Emotional State

For many authors, creativity feels unpredictable, tied to fleeting moments of inspiration or favorable emotional states. But what if creativity didn't have to rely on mood or circumstance? What if you could access your creative flow on demand, transforming even the most uninspired days into opportunities for productive writing?

This chapter provides a detailed guide to developing the mindset, techniques, and habits that enable you to summon creativity anytime, anywhere—no matter how you feel.

The Myth of "Waiting for Inspiration"

Creativity is often romanticized as a mysterious, uncontrollable force that strikes at random. While moments of sudden inspiration are exhilarating, they are rare and unreliable. Relying solely on these moments can lead to procrastination and inconsistency.

The truth is, creativity is a skill that can be cultivated and accessed intentionally. By shifting your mindset and employing practical techniques, you can transform creativity from a passive occurrence into an active process.

Understanding the Mechanics of Creativity

Creativity involves both the conscious and subconscious mind. The conscious mind gathers information, sets goals, and applies structure, while the subconscious mind generates ideas by connecting seemingly unrelated concepts. The interplay between these two systems is what fuels inspiration.

The key to tapping into creativity on demand is creating conditions that:

1. Stimulate your subconscious mind.
2. Provide structure and focus for your conscious efforts.

Techniques for Accessing Creativity on Demand

1. Establish a Creative Trigger

A creative trigger is a ritual or routine that signals to your brain it's time to enter a creative state.

How to Do It:

- Identify a consistent activity to perform before writing, such as lighting a candle, listening to a specific song, or making a cup of tea.
- Use the same location or tools for writing whenever possible to create a sense of familiarity and focus.
- Over time, your brain will associate the trigger with creative work, making it easier to shift into a creative mindset.

2. Use the "5-Minute Start" Rule

Starting can often be the hardest part of writing. The 5-minute rule helps you overcome inertia by committing to write for just five minutes.

How to Do It:

- Set a timer for five minutes and begin writing, no matter how you feel.
- If inspiration doesn't strike, write anything—stream-of-consciousness thoughts, observations about your surroundings, or even random words.
- Often, the act of starting is enough to unlock your creative flow, and you'll find yourself writing well beyond the initial five minutes.

3. Tap Into Your Subconscious with Mind Mapping

Mind mapping is a visual brainstorming technique that helps you generate ideas and connections.

How to Do It:

- Write a central concept or word in the middle of a page.
- Draw branches outward, adding related ideas, questions, or themes.
- Explore tangents freely, allowing your subconscious to make unexpected connections.

Why It Works:

Mind mapping engages both your creative and logical thinking, providing a structured yet flexible way to explore new ideas.

4. Shift Emotional States with Music or Movement

Your emotional state significantly impacts creativity. When you're feeling stuck or uninspired, music and movement can help you shift gears.

How to Do It:

- Create playlists tailored to different writing moods, such as upbeat tracks for energizing scenes or ambient music for reflective moments.
- Take a 5–10 minute movement break, such as dancing, stretching, or going for a brisk walk, to reset your mind and body.

Why It Works:

Music and movement stimulate dopamine production, which enhances focus, motivation, and creative thinking.

5. Leverage the Power of Constraints

Paradoxically, imposing limits on your writing can spark creativity by forcing you to think outside the box.

How to Do It:

- Set a word limit for a scene or a time limit for a writing session.
- Write a story or description using only a specific number of sentences or avoiding certain words.
- Experiment with unusual genres, formats, or perspectives.

Why It Works:

Constraints challenge your brain to find creative solutions, often leading to unexpected and innovative ideas.

6. Utilize the "What If?" Technique

"What if?" questions are a powerful way to generate ideas by imagining alternate possibilities or scenarios.

How to Do It:

- Ask open-ended questions like:
    - *What if my protagonist faced an unexpected betrayal?*
    - *What if this story were set in a different time period?*
    - *What if the rules of this world were reversed?*
- Explore answers without judgment, following the thread of each idea to see where it leads.

Why It Works:
This technique encourages curiosity and opens up new creative pathways.

7. Draw Inspiration from Real Life

Sometimes, the best ideas come from observing the world around you.

How to Do It:

- Spend time people-watching in public places, noting mannerisms, conversations, and interactions.
- Record interesting details, phrases, or events in a notebook or voice memo app.
- Reflect on personal experiences or memories that could serve as the foundation for a story.

Why It Works:
Real-life observations add authenticity and depth to your writing while providing a constant source of inspiration.

8. Access Flow State Through Focused Work

Flow state is the optimal state of consciousness for creativity, where focus is effortless, and ideas flow freely.

How to Do It:

- Eliminate distractions by turning off notifications and creating a dedicated writing space.
- Set clear, achievable goals for each session.
- Work in timed intervals, such as the Pomodoro Technique, to maintain focus without fatigue.

Why It Works:
Flow state enhances productivity and creativity by immersing you fully in the task at hand.

Building a Creative Infrastructure

To consistently access creativity on demand, it's essential to establish habits and systems that support your creative process over the long term.

1. Maintain a Creativity Journal

Keep a dedicated journal for capturing ideas, observations, and reflections. Review it regularly to find patterns and inspiration.

2. Prioritize Rest and Recovery

Creativity thrives when your mind and body are well-rested. Prioritize sleep, self-care, and downtime to recharge.

3. Create a Creativity Toolkit

Assemble a collection of resources that inspire you, such as favorite books, films, music, or visual art. Turn to these when you need a creative boost.

4. Practice Curiosity Daily

Adopt a mindset of curiosity by asking questions, seeking new experiences, and learning about unfamiliar topics. Curiosity fuels creative thinking.

Overcoming Emotional Blocks

Creativity often feels elusive when you're experiencing negative emotions like stress, sadness, or frustration. Here's how to navigate these challenges:

1. Write Through Emotions

Use writing as a tool to process and channel your emotions. Even if it doesn't directly relate to your project, it can clear mental and emotional space for creativity.

2. Reframe Negative Thoughts

Replace limiting beliefs like "I can't be creative right now" with empowering ones like "Creativity is always within me."

3. Use Visualization

Imagine yourself writing effortlessly, visualizing the scene, words, or ideas flowing freely. Visualization can help shift your mindset and prepare you for action.

Conclusion: Creativity Anytime, Anywhere

Creativity is not a mysterious force that appears only under ideal circumstances. It's a skill that can be accessed and strengthened through intentional practices and techniques. By implementing the strategies in this chapter, you'll gain the ability to summon creativity on demand, regardless of your emotional state or external environment.

Chapter 9: Visionary Thinking
How to Think Beyond the Present and Create Stories and Content That Impact Future Generations
Every author has the potential to leave a lasting legacy, crafting stories and ideas that transcend time and resonate with audiences long after the final page is turned. Visionary thinking is the ability to imagine a future shaped by your creativity, to craft stories and content that challenge norms, inspire change, and offer insights into the human experience. It's about seeing beyond the immediate and creating works that not only entertain but also endure.

This chapter explores the principles of visionary thinking, offering strategies to develop a forward-thinking mindset and create content that will impact future generations.

What Is Visionary Thinking?
Visionary thinking is the art of anticipating what could be rather than merely reacting to what is. It involves crafting stories and content that:

- **Address timeless themes:** Such as love, justice, identity, and resilience.
- **Incorporate universal truths:** Ideas that remain relevant regardless of cultural or temporal context.
- **Push boundaries:** Introducing new ideas, perspectives, or technologies that challenge conventional thinking.
- **Resonate emotionally:** Evoking feelings and connections that stand the test of time.

For authors, visionary thinking means going beyond trends and writing with a sense of purpose and foresight. It requires balancing relevance to the present with ideas that anticipate and influence the future.

The Importance of Visionary Content
Creating visionary content is not just about artistic ambition—it's about impact. Stories that endure inspire conversations, shape cultures, and spark innovation. Consider works like George Orwell's *1984*, Octavia Butler's *Parable of the Sower*, or Tolkien's *The Lord of the Rings*. These visionary pieces continue to influence literature, art, and societal discourse decades after their creation.

By thinking beyond the immediate, you can:

- Craft narratives that challenge societal norms or explore future possibilities.
- Position yourself as a thought leader whose work shapes cultural conversations.
- Leave a legacy that future generations will treasure and learn from.

Principles of Visionary Thinking
1. Focus on Universal Themes
Universal themes transcend time and culture, making your work relevant to a broad audience.
Action Steps:

- Identify themes in your writing that resonate universally, such as the quest for identity, the struggle for freedom, or the nature of love.
- Explore how these themes can be framed in new or innovative ways to connect with contemporary and future readers.

Examples:

- A sci-fi novel exploring freedom through the lens of AI rights.
- A fantasy epic delving into the human need for belonging and community.

2. Anticipate Future Trends and Challenges
Visionary works often predict or respond to the challenges of the future, from technological advancements to societal shifts.
Action Steps:

- Research emerging trends in science, technology, and culture. How might they shape the world 10, 20, or 50 years from now?
- Ask questions like: *What if climate change accelerates? How will AI redefine humanity? What new forms of conflict might arise?*
- Incorporate speculative elements that explore the implications of these trends.

Examples:

- A dystopian story imagining a world governed by corporations using personal data as currency.
- A utopian tale envisioning humanity's triumph over climate change through collective action.

3. Build Complex, Enduring Characters

Characters are the heart of any story. Visionary characters reflect universal truths while navigating unique, thought-provoking circumstances.

Action Steps:

- Create multi-dimensional characters with motivations, flaws, and growth arcs that resonate with readers.
- Place your characters in scenarios that test their values or challenge societal norms.
- Allow your characters to embody the struggles and hopes of humanity, making their journeys timeless.

Examples:

- A character who questions the morality of a utopian society built on hidden oppression.
- A protagonist who confronts their biases while forming unlikely alliances in a divided world.

4. Challenge Existing Norms

Visionary works often question the status quo, offering fresh perspectives or proposing alternative realities.

Action Steps:

- Identify societal norms, beliefs, or systems you want to challenge or explore.
- Use your writing to pose questions or present scenarios that invite readers to reconsider their assumptions.
- Balance critique with hope, offering solutions or paths forward rather than focusing solely on problems.

Examples:

- A novel critiquing consumer culture through a world where emotions are commodified.
- A short story imagining a society where empathy is the most valued trait.

5. Incorporate Diverse Perspectives

Visionary thinking embraces the complexity of human experience, including voices and perspectives often underrepresented in traditional narratives.

Action Steps:

- Research cultures, histories, and philosophies outside your own to enrich your work.
- Collaborate with or seek feedback from individuals with different backgrounds and experiences.
- Reflect on how diverse perspectives can illuminate universal themes or expand your narrative's scope.

Examples:

- A fantasy inspired by the folklore of underrepresented cultures.
- A futuristic tale exploring intersectionality in a post-gender society.

6. Blend Imagination with Research

Visionary content combines creative speculation with grounded, well-researched ideas to ensure plausibility and depth.

Action Steps:

- Immerse yourself in research related to your story's setting, themes, or technology.
- Use your findings as a foundation to build imaginative worlds or scenarios.
- Balance technical accuracy with creative freedom, ensuring your vision feels both innovative and authentic.

Examples:

- A novel about space colonization informed by current advancements in astrophysics.
- A speculative fiction story exploring genetic engineering's societal implications.

Practical Exercises for Visionary Thinking
1. Futurecasting Exercise

- Write a scene set 50 years in the future. Imagine how technology, society, and daily life might have evolved.
- Focus on how these changes affect your characters and their interactions.

2. The "What If?" Challenge

- Choose a current event, trend, or issue and project it into the future. Ask questions like:
    - *What if this issue intensifies?*
    - *What if humanity overcomes this challenge?*
    - *What unexpected consequences might arise?*

3. Reverse Worldbuilding

- Start with the legacy you want your story to leave behind. Ask:
    - *What do I want readers to feel or think?*
    - *What lessons or questions do I want my work to inspire?*
- Build your story's characters, plot, and themes to support that vision.

Examples of Visionary Storytelling
Margaret Atwood's *The Handmaid's Tale*
Explores themes of power, control, and gender dynamics, offering a cautionary tale with enduring relevance.
Isaac Asimov's *Foundation Series*
Blends advanced mathematics and human psychology to imagine the future of civilization, influencing generations of science fiction.
Octavia Butler's *Kindred*
Combines speculative fiction with historical insight, addressing themes of identity, race, and resilience in a way that resonates across time.
Creating a Legacy of Visionary Content
To leave a lasting impact:

- Write with purpose, crafting stories that challenge, inspire, and connect.
- Embrace experimentation, taking creative risks to push boundaries.
- Prioritize quality over speed, focusing on depth and substance.
- Share your work widely, ensuring it reaches the audiences who will carry it forward.

Conclusion: Thinking Beyond Today

Visionary thinking is a gift to both your readers and future generations. By crafting stories that address universal truths, challenge the status quo, and anticipate the future, you can create a legacy that endures. Your work has the power to inspire, provoke, and shape the world—not just today but for years to come.

Chapter 10: Storytelling Secrets

Mastering the Art of Storytelling to Engage, Inspire, and Sell

Storytelling is one of the oldest and most powerful forms of communication. It has the unique ability to captivate attention, evoke emotions, and inspire action. For authors, storytelling is not just a skill—it is the foundation of success. A well-told story can turn casual readers into devoted fans, transform abstract ideas into compelling narratives, and drive book sales by creating a lasting impact.

In this chapter, we will explore the secrets of storytelling mastery. You'll learn how to craft narratives that engage your audience, inspire deep emotional connections, and compel readers to share and support your work.

The Power of Storytelling

Why do stories matter so much? Humans are hardwired to respond to stories. Neuroscience shows that stories activate multiple regions of the brain, creating a deeply immersive experience. A good story can:

- **Capture attention:** Stories are more engaging than facts or data alone, making them memorable.
- **Evoke emotion:** Emotionally charged stories create a connection between the storyteller and the audience.
- **Inspire action:** Whether it's buying a book, sharing a message, or advocating for a cause, stories motivate people to act.

For authors, mastering storytelling is the key to creating work that resonates and succeeds in the marketplace.

The Core Elements of Great Storytelling
1. Relatable Characters

Compelling stories begin with characters that readers care about. Whether it's a hero, an anti-hero, or a supporting character, the audience must feel connected to their journey.

How to Create Relatable Characters:

- **Give them depth:** Flesh out their personality, backstory, motivations, and flaws.
- **Show their growth:** Allow characters to evolve as they face challenges and make choices.
- **Make them human:** Even extraordinary characters should have relatable traits, such as vulnerability, humor, or fear.

Example:
Harry Potter's bravery is inspiring, but it's his struggles with loneliness, self-doubt, and grief that make him relatable.

2. A Gripping Plot

A well-structured plot keeps readers engaged from beginning to end. It creates tension, raises questions, and delivers satisfying resolutions.

The Three-Act Structure:

- **Act 1: Setup**
    - Introduce the protagonist, their world, and the central conflict.
    - Hook the reader with an inciting incident that propels the story forward.
- **Act 2: Confrontation**
    - Develop the conflict through rising action and challenges.
    - Deepen character relationships and raise the stakes.
- **Act 3: Resolution**
    - Deliver a climax where the protagonist faces the ultimate test.
    - Resolve the conflict in a way that feels earned and meaningful.

Tips for a Gripping Plot:

- Use cliffhangers to keep readers turning pages.
- Include twists and surprises to subvert expectations.
- Balance pacing with moments of tension and relief.

3. Emotional Resonance

Emotion is the heart of storytelling. Readers may forget facts, but they will remember how a story made them feel.

How to Create Emotional Resonance:

- **Show, don't tell:** Instead of stating emotions, show them through actions, dialogue, and sensory details.
- **Use universal themes:** Themes like love, loss, hope, and redemption evoke strong emotions.
- **Tap into contrasts:** Juxtapose joy and sorrow, success and failure, or safety and danger to heighten emotional impact.

Example:

In *The Fault in Our Stars*, John Green explores love and loss through relatable characters, creating a story that deeply moves readers.

4. A Clear Message or Theme

Great stories have something to say. A theme or central message gives your narrative purpose and resonance.

How to Incorporate Themes:

- Identify the core question or idea your story explores. For example: *What does it mean to be truly free?*
- Weave the theme into character arcs, plot developments, and subtext.
- Avoid being overly didactic; let readers uncover the theme through the story's events and characters.

5. Vivid Worldbuilding

For stories set in fantastical or unfamiliar settings, immersive worldbuilding is essential.

How to Build a Believable World:

- Establish rules: Define the logic, history, and culture of your world.
- Use sensory details: Describe sights, sounds, smells, tastes, and textures to make the world tangible.
- Integrate worldbuilding naturally: Avoid info-dumps; reveal details through dialogue, action, or context.

Example:

J.R.R. Tolkien's *Middle-earth* is a masterclass in worldbuilding, with rich histories, languages, and cultures that bring the setting to life.

Advanced Storytelling Techniques
1. The Power of Subtext

Subtext is the unspoken or implied meaning beneath the surface of a story. It adds depth and engages readers by encouraging interpretation.

Examples of Subtext:

- A character's body language revealing their true feelings.
- Dialogue that hints at hidden motives or secrets.

2. The Hero's Journey

Joseph Campbell's "Hero's Journey" is a timeless narrative structure that resonates deeply with audiences.

Key Stages:

- The Call to Adventure: The protagonist is drawn into a new world or challenge.
- Trials and Tribulations: They face obstacles that test their resolve.
- Transformation: They emerge changed, gaining wisdom, strength, or clarity.

3. Foreshadowing and Symbolism

Foreshadowing hints at future events, creating anticipation, while symbolism adds layers of meaning to a story.

How to Use These Tools:

- Foreshadowing: Drop subtle clues that set up future revelations or twists.
- Symbolism: Use objects, colors, or motifs to represent themes or character arcs.

Storytelling for Marketing and Selling

Storytelling is not only a tool for crafting books but also for marketing and selling them.

1. Tell the Story of Your Book

- Share the inspiration behind your story to connect with potential readers.
- Highlight the themes, characters, or emotions that make your book unique.

2. Use Storytelling in Marketing Materials

- Craft engaging blurbs, synopses, and taglines that hook readers.
- Create visual stories through book trailers, social media posts, or promotional videos.

3. Build a Personal Narrative as an Author

- Share your journey as a writer to build authenticity and rapport with your audience.
- Use storytelling to convey your passion and purpose, inspiring readers to support your work.

Practical Exercises to Master Storytelling

1. Rewrite a Classic Story

- Take a well-known tale and retell it from a different perspective or setting. This exercise helps you understand narrative structure and character development.

2. Analyze Your Favorite Stories

- Identify the elements that make them compelling. What hooks you? What emotional beats resonate most?

3. Write a Micro-Story

- Craft a complete story in 500 words or less. Focus on a single moment, conflict, or transformation.

Conclusion: The Storyteller's Legacy

Mastering storytelling is more than a technical skill—it's an art that allows you to connect with readers on a profound level. By applying the principles and techniques in this chapter, you can craft narratives that engage, inspire, and sell, ensuring your stories leave a lasting impact.

Part III: The Productivity Powerhouse

Chapter 11: Time Bending

Maximizing Productivity Using Time-Management Hacks to Get More Done in Less Time

In today's fast-paced world, time is the ultimate currency. For authors balancing creative endeavors with daily responsibilities, managing time effectively can be the difference between achieving goals and feeling perpetually overwhelmed. Time bending is about mastering the art of productivity—not by creating more hours in a day but by using the ones you have with unparalleled efficiency.

This chapter provides proven time-management hacks and strategies tailored for authors, enabling you to maximize productivity, maintain creative flow, and achieve more in less time.

The Importance of Time Bending for Authors

Writing demands both sustained focus and imaginative freedom. Yet, competing priorities—day jobs, family obligations, marketing tasks, or self-doubt—can eat away at precious writing time. Time bending allows you to:

- **Prioritize effectively:** Focus on what truly matters without getting bogged down by distractions.
- **Eliminate wasted time:** Identify and minimize habits or activities that don't contribute to your goals.
- **Protect creative energy:** Allocate your peak mental hours to high-value tasks like writing or brainstorming.

By mastering time bending, you take control of your schedule rather than letting it control you.

The Principles of Time Bending

1. The Pareto Principle (80/20 Rule)

The Pareto Principle states that 80% of results come from 20% of efforts. Identify the 20% of tasks that have the most impact on your writing goals and focus on those.

Examples for Authors:

- Writing quality pages matters more than perfecting the format of a book proposal.
- Engaging with your target audience matters more than posting on every social media platform.

2. The Eisenhower Matrix

This tool helps you prioritize tasks based on urgency and importance.

How to Use It:

- **Urgent and Important:** Focus on these first (e.g., meeting a deadline).
- **Important but Not Urgent:** Schedule these (e.g., developing a new book idea).
- **Urgent but Not Important:** Delegate or minimize (e.g., routine admin tasks).
- **Not Urgent and Not Important:** Eliminate or postpone (e.g., excessive scrolling on social media).

3. Parkinson's Law

Parkinson's Law states that tasks expand to fill the time available for their completion. By setting shorter deadlines, you can increase focus and efficiency.

Examples for Authors:

- Commit to writing 500 words in 30 minutes rather than "sometime today."
- Limit research to a specific time block to avoid getting lost in rabbit holes.

Time Bending Hacks for Authors

1. Create a Writing Routine

Establishing a consistent routine reduces decision fatigue and helps you build momentum.

How to Implement It:

- Set aside a dedicated time each day for writing, even if it's just 30 minutes.
- Create a pre-writing ritual, such as lighting a candle, making tea, or reviewing notes, to signal your brain it's time to focus.
- Protect this time by treating it as non-negotiable.

2. Use the Pomodoro Technique

This method boosts productivity by breaking work into focused intervals with short breaks.

How It Works:

- Set a timer for 25 minutes and focus on writing.
- Take a 5-minute break.
- Repeat this cycle four times, then take a longer 15–30-minute break.

Why It Works:

Short, intense bursts of focus prevent burnout and help you maintain concentration.

3. Batch Similar Tasks

Batching involves grouping similar tasks together to reduce the cognitive load of switching between activities.

Examples:

- Write all your social media posts for the week in one session.
- Dedicate a specific day to editing, another to outlining, and another to marketing tasks.
- Handle emails or administrative work during a designated time block.

4. Identify and Leverage Peak Productivity Hours

Your energy and focus fluctuate throughout the day. Identify your peak hours and schedule your most demanding tasks during that time.

How to Find Your Peak Hours:

- Track your energy and focus levels over several days.
- Notice when you feel most creative and alert.
- Reserve these hours for writing or brainstorming, leaving lower-energy tasks for other times.

5. Outsource or Delegate

If certain tasks drain your time or energy without contributing directly to your goals, consider outsourcing them.

Examples for Authors:

- Hire a virtual assistant for administrative work or social media management.
- Use freelance services for book cover design, formatting, or editing.
- Automate repetitive tasks, such as scheduling posts or tracking expenses.

6. Limit Decision Fatigue

The more decisions you make, the harder it becomes to focus on creative work. Simplify your life to conserve mental energy.

How to Reduce Decision Fatigue:

- Plan your day in advance, including meals and outfits.
- Use templates or checklists for recurring tasks like outlining a story or sending query letters.
- Stick to a writing schedule to avoid deciding "when" to write.

7. Practice the Two-Minute Rule

If a task takes less than two minutes to complete, do it immediately rather than postponing it.

Examples:

- Respond to a quick email.
- Organize your writing desk.
- Write a reminder or note for later reference.

Why It Works:

Small tasks often take longer to manage if delayed than to complete immediately.

8. Block Distractions

Distractions are the enemy of productivity. Minimize interruptions to protect your focus.

Action Steps:

- Use apps like Freedom or Focus@Will to block social media or distracting websites.
- Silence notifications during writing sessions.
- Create a distraction-free environment by tidying your workspace and informing others of your writing schedule.

Tools and Technology to Enhance Time Bending
1. Writing Software

- **Scrivener:** Organize large projects and keep notes, outlines, and drafts in one place.
- **Ulysses:** A distraction-free writing app with robust organizational tools.

2. Task Management Apps

- **Trello:** Visualize tasks and projects with drag-and-drop boards.
- **Asana:** Track progress on multiple writing or marketing projects.

3. Calendar and Scheduling Tools

- **Google Calendar:** Schedule writing blocks and reminders.
- **Time Blocking Apps:** Plan your day hour-by-hour for maximum focus.

4. Productivity Timers

- **Forest:** Stay focused by growing a virtual tree during productive sessions.
- **TomatoTimer:** A simple Pomodoro Technique timer.

Avoiding Common Time Management Pitfalls
1. Overcommitting
Taking on too many projects can lead to burnout and reduced productivity. Learn to say no to tasks that don't align with your goals.
2. Perfectionism
Perfectionism can slow you down and prevent you from completing tasks. Aim for progress, not perfection.
3. Ignoring Self-Care
Time bending is ineffective if you're constantly exhausted or unmotivated. Prioritize rest, nutrition, and physical activity to sustain productivity.
Creating Your Personal Time-Bending System

1. **Identify Priorities:** Clarify your writing and career goals to determine which tasks matter most.
2. **Plan Ahead:** Use weekly and daily planning to allocate time for high-impact activities.
3. **Adapt and Reflect:** Regularly review your schedule and adjust as needed to stay aligned with your goals.

Conclusion: Making Every Minute Count

Time bending isn't about working harder—it's about working smarter. By mastering time-management hacks and implementing the strategies in this chapter, you can maximize your productivity, protect your creative energy, and make meaningful progress toward your goals.

Chapter 12: Focus Mastery

Training Your Brain to Focus Deeply Despite Distractions

In an age of constant interruptions—social media notifications, endless emails, and the daily barrage of responsibilities—focus has become one of the most valuable skills an author can possess. Deep focus, the ability to concentrate fully on a task without distraction, is the cornerstone of productivity and creativity. It allows you to write with clarity, solve complex problems, and enter a state of flow where your best work emerges.

This chapter provides actionable techniques to train your brain for focus mastery, enabling you to write and create deeply even in a world filled with distractions.

The Importance of Deep Focus for Authors

1. Enhanced Creativity

Deep focus allows your mind to make connections and generate ideas that surface only when you're fully immersed in your work.

2. Increased Productivity

When you focus deeply, you accomplish more in less time, reducing stress and freeing up energy for other activities.

3. Greater Quality

Distractions lead to mistakes and fragmented thinking. Deep focus helps you produce polished, thoughtful work.

4. Access to Flow State

Flow state is the optimal mental state for creativity and productivity, achieved when you're completely absorbed in a task. Deep focus is the gateway to this state.

The Science of Focus

Focus is a mental skill influenced by neurobiology and environment. It involves:

- **The Prefrontal Cortex:** Responsible for decision-making, attention, and problem-solving.
- **Dopamine Regulation:** Dopamine drives motivation and reward, enhancing focus when appropriately balanced.
- **Neuroplasticity:** The brain's ability to adapt and strengthen focus-related pathways through practice.

Distractions derail focus by overstimulating the brain and triggering the release of stress hormones like cortisol. Training your brain to focus involves creating habits, routines, and environments that minimize distractions and reinforce sustained attention.

Barriers to Focus and How to Overcome Them

1. Digital Distractions

Smartphones, notifications, and constant connectivity are major obstacles to deep focus.

Solutions:

- **Turn off notifications:** Silence alerts on your phone and computer during writing sessions.
- **Use productivity apps:** Tools like Freedom or Cold Turkey block distracting websites.
- **Create phone-free zones:** Keep your phone in another room while writing.

2. Multitasking

The myth of multitasking reduces efficiency and focus, as the brain cannot fully engage with multiple tasks simultaneously.

Solutions:

- Commit to single-tasking by focusing on one activity at a time.
- Prioritize tasks using time-blocking or the Pomodoro Technique.
- Schedule specific times for secondary tasks like checking email.

3. Mental Clutter

Worries, to-do lists, and unorganized thoughts can pull your attention away from writing.

Solutions:

- Practice mindfulness meditation to clear your mind and improve present-moment focus.
- Use journaling to offload thoughts before starting work.
- Break large tasks into smaller, manageable steps to reduce overwhelm.

4. Lack of Energy

Fatigue, poor nutrition, and stress make it difficult to concentrate.

Solutions:

- Prioritize sleep, aiming for 7–9 hours per night.
- Eat brain-boosting foods like nuts, fish, and leafy greens.
- Exercise regularly to improve blood flow and cognitive function.

Training Your Brain for Deep Focus
1. Build a Focus Ritual
A pre-work ritual signals to your brain that it's time to concentrate.
Steps to Create a Ritual:

- Set a specific time and place for writing each day.
- Begin with a calming activity, like deep breathing, stretching, or reviewing your notes.
- Eliminate distractions by clearing your workspace and closing unrelated tabs or apps.

Example Ritual:

1. Brew a cup of tea.
2. Review your writing goals for the day.
3. Set a timer and begin.

2. Practice Mindfulness Meditation
Mindfulness strengthens attention by training you to focus on the present moment.
How to Practice:

- Sit in a quiet space and close your eyes.
- Focus on your breath, noticing the sensation of inhaling and exhaling.
- When your mind wanders, gently bring your attention back to your breath.

Start Small:

- Begin with 5 minutes a day and gradually increase to 20 minutes.

3. Use the Pomodoro Technique
This time-management method enhances focus by alternating work and rest periods.
How It Works:

- Set a timer for 25 minutes and work on a single task.
- Take a 5-minute break.
- Repeat for four cycles, then take a longer 15–30-minute break.

Why It Works:
The short bursts of focus prevent mental fatigue and help you maintain consistent attention.

4. Strengthen Your Focus Muscle with Attention Training
Just like physical fitness, focus improves with regular practice.

Exercises:

- **Focus on One Word:** Choose a single word, like "create," and concentrate on it for 1–5 minutes.
- **Count Backward:** Count backward from 100 by threes to sharpen your mental precision.
- **Observation Practice:** Spend 5 minutes observing a scene or object, noting every detail.

5. Optimize Your Workspace for Focus
A well-organized, distraction-free environment enhances concentration.

Steps to Optimize Your Space:

- Keep your workspace tidy and uncluttered.
- Use noise-canceling headphones or ambient sound apps like Noisli to block distractions.
- Adjust lighting and seating to ensure comfort without inducing sleepiness.

6. Embrace Deep Work Blocks
Deep work blocks are extended periods of uninterrupted focus on meaningful tasks.

How to Implement:

- Schedule 2–3 hours of deep work during your peak productivity hours.
- Turn off all notifications and minimize interruptions.
- Set a clear goal for each block, such as completing a chapter or outlining a scene.

7. Reward Focused Effort
Positive reinforcement motivates your brain to sustain focus over time.

How to Create Rewards:

- Set milestones, such as completing a page, and reward yourself with a small treat or break.
- Use larger rewards, like a favorite meal or leisure activity, for bigger accomplishments.

Strategies to Maintain Focus Despite Interruptions

1. Use the "Not Now" Technique

When distractions arise, acknowledge them and defer action.

How to Do It:

- Keep a notepad nearby to jot down distracting thoughts or tasks.
- Return to them after your focus session is complete.

2. Practice Self-Compassion

If you lose focus, avoid self-criticism. Gently redirect your attention to the task at hand.

Why It Works:

Self-compassion reduces stress, allowing you to refocus more quickly.

3. Train Others to Respect Your Focus Time

Inform family, friends, or coworkers of your focus periods and set boundaries to minimize interruptions.

The Long-Term Benefits of Focus Mastery

- **Increased Productivity:** Accomplish more in less time.
- **Improved Creativity:** Generate ideas and insights that arise from sustained focus.
- **Enhanced Well-Being:** Reduced stress and a sense of accomplishment.
- **Greater Consistency:** Build a reliable habit of deep work.

Conclusion: Mastering Focus in a Distracted World

Focus mastery is not a one-time achievement—it's a skill that requires consistent practice and intentional effort. By implementing the techniques in this chapter, you can train your brain to focus deeply despite distractions, unlocking your full potential as a writer and creator.

Chapter 13: Building Productive Habits

Creating Long-Term Habits That Guarantee Consistent Writing Output

Consistency is the secret ingredient behind every successful writer. While bursts of inspiration can lead to brilliant work, it's the daily, disciplined effort of productive habits that ensures long-term output and growth. Building habits isn't just about writing more—it's about creating a sustainable system that makes writing a natural and effortless part of your routine.

In this chapter, we will explore how to design and implement productive habits tailored to your goals, guaranteeing consistent writing output and paving the way for enduring success.

Why Habits Matter for Writers

1. They Reduce Mental Effort

Habits turn intentional actions into automatic behaviors, conserving mental energy for creativity.

2. They Build Momentum

Small, consistent actions accumulate over time, leading to significant progress.

3. They Foster Discipline Over Motivation

Motivation is fleeting, but habits ensure you keep writing even when you don't feel inspired.

4. They Create Predictability

A structured routine eliminates uncertainty and helps you consistently carve out time for writing.

The Science of Habit Formation

Habits are formed through a cycle known as the **Habit Loop**, which consists of:

1. **Cue:** A trigger that initiates the behavior (e.g., a specific time, location, or activity).
2. **Routine:** The behavior itself (e.g., writing 500 words).
3. **Reward:** A positive reinforcement that encourages the repetition of the behavior (e.g., a sense of accomplishment or a small treat).

To build productive habits, you must:

- Identify effective cues.
- Design routines that align with your writing goals.
- Create meaningful rewards to reinforce the habit.

Steps to Building Productive Writing Habits

1. Start Small and Specific

Ambitious goals can feel overwhelming, leading to procrastination. Start with manageable actions that are easy to sustain.

Examples:

- Write for 10 minutes a day instead of aiming for hours.
- Commit to writing one sentence or paragraph daily to build momentum.

Why It Works:

Small, consistent actions build confidence and establish the foundation for larger habits.

2. Set Clear Goals

Vague intentions like "I'll write more" lack the clarity needed for habit formation. Define specific, measurable goals.

Examples:

- Write 500 words per day.
- Complete one chapter per week.
- Spend 30 minutes daily on editing.

Tips for Success:

- Use the SMART framework (Specific, Measurable, Achievable, Relevant, Time-bound) to set goals.
- Break larger projects into smaller milestones to make progress feel achievable.

3. Create a Writing Schedule

A consistent writing schedule establishes a routine that reinforces the habit.

How to Create One:

- Choose a specific time of day when you're most productive or least distracted.
- Block this time on your calendar as non-negotiable.
- Align your schedule with your natural energy levels (e.g., morning for early risers, evening for night owls).

4. Use Habit Stacking

Habit stacking involves pairing a new habit with an existing one to create a seamless routine.

Examples:

- Write for 20 minutes after your morning coffee.
- Edit your work immediately after finishing dinner.
- Outline a scene during your lunch break.

Why It Works:
By linking writing to an established habit, you create a stronger cue that reinforces the new behavior.

5. Remove Barriers to Writing

Identify and eliminate obstacles that make it difficult to write consistently.

Strategies:

- Keep your writing tools accessible (e.g., notebook, laptop, or app).
- Organize your workspace to minimize distractions.
- Use writing software that simplifies the process, like Scrivener or Google Docs.
- Create a distraction-free environment by silencing notifications and closing unrelated tabs.

6. Build Accountability

Accountability provides external motivation to stick to your habits.

How to Build Accountability:

- Join a writing group or community where members share goals and progress.
- Partner with an accountability buddy who checks in on your writing routine.
- Announce your goals publicly on social media or to friends and family.

7. Track Your Progress

Tracking reinforces habits by providing tangible evidence of your achievements.

Tools to Use:

- Journals or planners to log daily word counts or writing sessions.
- Apps like Trello or Notion to track milestones and goals.
- Habit-tracking apps like Habitica or Streaks to visualize consistency.

Why It Works:
Seeing progress motivates you to keep going and highlights patterns that need adjustment.

8. Celebrate Small Wins
Rewards create positive reinforcement, making it more likely you'll repeat the behavior.
Examples of Rewards:

- Enjoy a favorite snack after reaching a daily word count.
- Take a break to watch an episode of a show after completing a chapter.
- Treat yourself to new writing supplies after achieving a major milestone.

Why It Works:
Celebrating progress creates a sense of achievement, encouraging consistency.

9. Prepare for Setbacks
Habits take time to solidify, and setbacks are part of the process. Planning for challenges ensures you stay on track.
How to Overcome Setbacks:

- Forgive yourself if you miss a day; focus on restarting the habit as soon as possible.
- Identify triggers that disrupt your routine and develop strategies to counteract them.
- Adjust your goals if they feel too ambitious or unsustainable.

Examples of Productive Writing Habits

1. **Daily Freewriting**
    - Write freely for 10 minutes every morning to warm up your creativity.
    - Focus on ideas, scenes, or reflections without worrying about quality.
2. **Weekly Writing Sessions**
    - Dedicate two extended sessions per week to deep work, such as completing drafts or major edits.
3. **End-of-Day Reviews**
    - Reflect on your progress each evening, noting accomplishments and setting intentions for the next day.
4. **Pre-Writing Rituals**
    - Develop a routine that prepares your mind for writing, such as journaling, meditating, or reviewing notes.

Long-Term Strategies for Sustaining Writing Habits

1. Periodically Review and Adjust

Habits evolve as your goals and circumstances change. Regularly assess your routines to ensure they remain effective.

2. Align Habits with Your Vision

Connect your daily habits to your larger goals, such as completing a novel or publishing a book. This creates a sense of purpose and direction.

3. Avoid Overloading Yourself

Focus on one or two habits at a time. Overloading can lead to burnout and undermine consistency.

4. Seek Inspiration Regularly

Incorporate activities that fuel your creativity, such as reading, attending events, or exploring new ideas.

The Power of Consistent Writing Output

Small, consistent actions can lead to extraordinary results over time. For example:

- Writing just 500 words a day adds up to 182,500 words in a year—enough for multiple books.
- Consistent habit-building improves not only productivity but also skill and confidence.

Conclusion: The Habit of Success

Building productive habits is the foundation of consistent writing output. By starting small, staying accountable, and celebrating progress, you can create a sustainable routine that transforms writing from a sporadic activity into a lifelong practice.

Chapter 14: Navigating Distractions

How to Eliminate Distractions, Digital or Physical, from Your Writing Space

In the modern world, distractions are everywhere. From buzzing smartphones to cluttered desks, interruptions can derail even the most focused author. The ability to eliminate distractions and maintain concentration is a superpower that can dramatically enhance your productivity and creativity.

This chapter provides a comprehensive guide to identifying, managing, and eliminating distractions—both digital and physical—so you can create a writing space that fosters deep focus and consistent output.

The Impact of Distractions on Writing

Distractions can have a ripple effect on your writing process:

1. **Loss of Focus:** Switching tasks fragments your attention, making it harder to enter a state of flow.
2. **Decreased Productivity:** Constant interruptions mean spending more time regaining focus than actually writing.
3. **Reduced Creativity:** Distractions limit the mental bandwidth needed for innovative thinking and storytelling.
4. **Increased Stress:** Feeling unproductive due to distractions leads to frustration and self-doubt.

By learning to navigate and eliminate distractions, you can reclaim your time and creative energy.

Step 1: Identify Your Distractions

The first step in eliminating distractions is recognizing their sources. These typically fall into two categories:

1. Digital Distractions

- Social media notifications.
- Emails and instant messages.
- Endless tabs and apps.
- Smartphone alerts and calls.

2. Physical Distractions

- A cluttered or disorganized workspace.
- Noise from family members, roommates, or the environment.
- Uncomfortable seating, lighting, or desk setup.
- Interruptions from pets, children, or visitors.

Step 2: Eliminate Digital Distractions

Digital distractions are among the most pervasive challenges for modern writers. Here's how to address them:

1. Set Boundaries for Technology

- **Turn Off Notifications:** Silence alerts on your phone and computer during writing sessions.
- **Use Focus Modes:** Activate "Do Not Disturb" or "Focus Mode" on your devices to block interruptions.
- **Schedule Digital Check-Ins:** Allocate specific times for checking email and social media, and stick to them.

2. Use Productivity Tools

- **Website Blockers:** Apps like Freedom, StayFocusd, or Cold Turkey can block access to distracting websites during writing hours.
- **Pomodoro Timers:** Tools like TomatoTimer or Forest help you stay focused in 25-minute intervals.
- **Writing Software:** Use distraction-free writing tools like Scrivener, Ulysses, or FocusWriter to minimize on-screen clutter.

3. Create a Separate Writing Device

- If possible, use a device dedicated to writing, free of unnecessary apps or distractions.
- Consider disabling Wi-Fi or using airplane mode during writing sessions.

Step 3: Optimize Your Physical Environment
Your physical workspace plays a significant role in your ability to focus.
1. Declutter Your Space

- **Remove Non-Essentials:** Keep only the tools you need for writing—your computer, notebook, pen, and any reference materials.
- **Organize Materials:** Store notes, books, and resources in designated areas to avoid visual clutter.
- **Create a Clean Surface:** A tidy desk helps clear your mind and reduces distractions.

2. Control Noise Levels

- **Use Noise-Canceling Headphones:** Block out external noise with music, white noise, or ambient sound apps like Noisli or Rainy Mood.
- **Choose Quiet Hours:** Write during times when your environment is naturally quieter, such as early morning or late evening.
- **Communicate Boundaries:** Let family or roommates know your writing schedule to minimize interruptions.

3. Improve Comfort and Ergonomics

- **Invest in a Comfortable Chair:** Proper back support can prevent discomfort that distracts from writing.
- **Adjust Lighting:** Use soft, warm lighting to reduce eye strain and create a relaxing atmosphere.
- **Set Up Your Desk Properly:** Position your screen at eye level and maintain a comfortable distance from your keyboard.

Step 4: Manage Interruptions from Others

People are one of the most common sources of distractions. Set clear boundaries to protect your writing time.

1. Set Expectations

- **Communicate Your Schedule:** Share your writing hours with family, friends, or roommates.
- **Use Visual Signals:** A closed door, a "Do Not Disturb" sign, or headphones can signal that you're unavailable.

2. Be Firm but Kind

- Politely remind others of your need for uninterrupted time.
- Offer alternatives, such as scheduling time to address their concerns after your writing session.

3. Create a Backup Plan

- If interruptions are unavoidable, have a secondary writing space you can retreat to, such as a library or café.

Step 5: Train Your Mind to Resist Internal Distractions

Internal distractions, like daydreaming, self-doubt, or worrying, can be just as disruptive as external ones.

1. Practice Mindfulness

- Use meditation to train your mind to focus on the present moment.
- When your mind wanders, gently redirect your attention to your writing.

2. Use the "Not Now" Technique

- Keep a notebook nearby to jot down intrusive thoughts or unrelated ideas that pop up during writing.
- Revisit these notes after your session to avoid derailing your focus.

3. Address Negative Self-Talk

- Replace thoughts like "I'll never finish this" with affirmations like "I am making progress with each word I write."
- Acknowledge and challenge doubts to keep them from becoming distractions.

Step 6: Establish Routines That Reinforce Focus
Routines help create structure and minimize decision fatigue, making it easier to concentrate.

1. Create a Writing Ritual

- Begin each session with a consistent activity, such as reviewing your outline, making tea, or lighting a candle.
- A ritual signals to your brain that it's time to focus.

2. Schedule Writing Blocks

- Dedicate specific time blocks for writing, prioritizing hours when you're most productive.
- Use time-blocking to reserve uninterrupted periods for deep work.

3. End with a Transition

- Conclude each session with a brief reflection or goal-setting activity to transition out of writing mode.

Step 7: Test and Adapt Your Strategies
No single approach works for everyone. Experiment with different techniques to discover what suits your personality and environment.

Tips for Testing:

- Try new tools or strategies for at least a week to assess their effectiveness.
- Adjust your approach based on your schedule, energy levels, and feedback from others.

Tools and Resources to Eliminate Distractions
1. Digital Tools

- **Freedom:** Block distracting websites and apps.
- **RescueTime:** Track how you spend your time online and identify productivity pitfalls.
- **Forest:** Stay focused by growing a virtual tree during uninterrupted work sessions.

2. Physical Aids

- **Noise-Canceling Headphones:** Ideal for blocking out background noise.
- **Standing Desks:** Encourage movement and reduce discomfort during long writing sessions.
- **Bullet Journals:** Help track goals and stay organized.

Benefits of a Distraction-Free Writing Space

- **Increased Productivity:** Spend more time writing and less time regaining focus.
- **Improved Creativity:** Uninterrupted time fosters deeper thinking and imaginative breakthroughs.
- **Reduced Stress:** A streamlined environment and routine create a sense of control and calm.
- **Consistent Output:** A distraction-free space ensures regular progress on your writing goals.

Conclusion: Designing Your Ideal Writing Space

Eliminating distractions is about creating an environment and mindset that support your writing. By addressing both digital and physical distractions, setting boundaries, and developing habits that reinforce focus, you can transform your writing space into a sanctuary for creativity and productivity.

Chapter 15: Flow State Activation

Techniques to Enter and Sustain Flow State for Peak Creative Productivity

The flow state is often described as the holy grail of productivity and creativity. It is that magical zone where time seems to disappear, distractions fade away, and ideas flow effortlessly. For authors, achieving flow is not just about writing faster—it's about accessing deeper creativity, crafting more inspired prose, and producing high-quality work.

This chapter delves into the science of flow state, exploring proven techniques to help you enter and sustain this optimal mental state, allowing you to unlock your full creative potential.

What Is Flow State?

Flow state, a term popularized by psychologist Mihaly Csikszentmihalyi, is a mental condition in which a person is fully immersed in a task, experiencing heightened focus, creativity, and performance.

Key Characteristics of Flow State:

1. **Intense Concentration:** Full focus on the task at hand.
2. **Effortless Action:** A sense that the work is unfolding naturally without struggle.
3. **Loss of Time Awareness:** Hours can pass without you noticing.
4. **Intrinsic Motivation:** The work feels deeply rewarding and meaningful.
5. **Reduced Self-Consciousness:** Focus shifts away from self-doubt or external concerns.

The Science Behind Flow State

Flow occurs when your skills are perfectly matched to a challenge—neither too easy (causing boredom) nor too hard (causing frustration). The brain releases dopamine, a neurotransmitter that enhances focus and motivation, creating the optimal conditions for creative problem-solving.

Triggers for Flow State:

1. **Clear Goals:** Knowing what you're trying to achieve eliminates mental clutter.
2. **Immediate Feedback:** Recognizing progress as you work helps sustain focus.
3. **Intense Focus:** Minimizing distractions allows your brain to fully engage with the task.

Step 1: Prepare Your Environment for Flow

Your surroundings play a significant role in facilitating flow.

1. Eliminate Distractions

- Turn off notifications on your phone and computer.
- Use tools like Freedom or StayFocusd to block distracting websites.
- Inform family or roommates of your writing schedule to minimize interruptions.

2. Optimize Your Workspace

- Keep your desk clean and organized to reduce visual distractions.
- Adjust lighting to a comfortable level—soft lighting can enhance focus.
- Use noise-canceling headphones or listen to ambient sounds or instrumental music.

3. Gather Your Tools

- Have everything you need within reach—notes, outlines, or research materials—so you don't break focus searching for them.

Step 2: Prime Your Mind for Flow
Your mental state is as important as your physical environment.
1. Set Clear Goals

- Define what you want to accomplish in your writing session, such as completing a scene or reaching a specific word count.
- Break larger goals into smaller, actionable steps to make progress feel manageable.

2. Visualize Success

- Spend a few minutes visualizing yourself writing effortlessly and achieving your goal.
- Imagine the satisfaction of finishing your session with a sense of accomplishment.

3. Use a Pre-Work Ritual

- Develop a consistent routine that signals to your brain it's time to focus, such as making tea, journaling for a few minutes, or reviewing your outline.

4. Manage Stress

- High stress levels can hinder flow. Use mindfulness or breathing exercises to calm your mind before starting.

Step 3: Techniques to Enter Flow State
1. Start with a Warm-Up
Ease into flow by engaging in a short, low-pressure activity related to your writing.
Examples:

- Freewriting for 5–10 minutes.
- Reviewing your notes or previous drafts.
- Writing a quick summary of the scene you're about to work on.

2. Match Challenge to Skill
Ensure your writing task is challenging enough to engage you but not so difficult that it becomes overwhelming.
How to Adjust:

- If the task feels too easy, add complexity by focusing on nuanced character development or vivid descriptions.
- If the task feels too hard, simplify it by focusing on smaller sections or bullet-pointing ideas.

3. Use Timed Writing Sessions
Set a timer to create a sense of urgency and focus.
Examples:

- Use the Pomodoro Technique: Write for 25 minutes, followed by a 5-minute break.
- Gradually increase your writing intervals as you build focus.

Step 4: Sustain Flow State
Once you've entered flow, maintaining it requires effort and awareness.
1. Resist Multitasking

- Focus on one task at a time to maintain deep concentration.
- Use tools to manage distracting thoughts, such as a notepad to jot down unrelated ideas for later.

2. Monitor Your Energy Levels

- Take breaks before fatigue sets in to prevent burnout.
- Stay hydrated and fuel your body with healthy snacks to maintain focus.

3. Embrace Imperfection

- Avoid self-editing during flow—focus on getting words down and refine later.
- Trust the process, knowing you can revisit and improve your work during editing.

Step 5: Enhance Flow with Proven Strategies
1. Leverage Music and Sound

- Instrumental music, nature sounds, or white noise can block distractions and enhance focus.
- Experiment with playlists tailored for focus, such as lo-fi beats or classical music.

2. Use Brainwave Entrainment

- Apps like Brain.fm or binaural beats claim to help you enter flow by syncing brainwaves to optimal frequencies.

3. Incorporate Movement

- Short physical activities, like stretching or a quick walk, can reset your mind and enhance flow when you return to writing.

4. Track Your Flow Patterns

- Keep a journal to note when and how you achieve flow.

- Identify patterns in your most productive sessions, such as time of day or specific rituals.

Step 6: Overcome Common Barriers to Flow
1. Fear of Failure

- Reframe failure as a natural part of the creative process.
- Focus on progress rather than perfection.

2. Interruptions

- Use a "Do Not Disturb" sign or block off your writing time on your calendar.
- Schedule writing sessions during quieter times of the day.

3. Lack of Motivation

- Remind yourself of your "why" by reflecting on your goals or the impact you want your writing to have.
- Reward yourself after completing a session to reinforce positive habits.

Flow State and Creativity: A Perfect Partnership

Flow state isn't just about productivity—it's about accessing the highest levels of creativity. When you're in flow:

- Your brain makes connections between ideas more easily.
- You're less likely to second-guess yourself, allowing for bold and innovative thinking.
- You produce work that feels authentic and inspired.

The Long-Term Benefits of Flow State Activation

- **Higher Output:** Consistently enter flow to complete projects faster without sacrificing quality.
- **Deeper Satisfaction:** Writing in flow feels fulfilling and energizing, reducing burnout.
- **Enhanced Skills:** Regular practice in flow helps refine your craft as a writer.

Conclusion: The Gateway to Your Best Work

Mastering flow state activation is not just a technique—it's a transformative practice that can elevate your writing and creative potential. By preparing your environment, priming your mind, and using proven techniques to enter and sustain flow, you can achieve peak productivity and create work that truly resonates.

Part IV: The Financial Freedom Blueprint

Chapter 16: Monetizing Your Craft

Unique Strategies for Turning Writing into a Highly Profitable Career

Turning your passion for writing into a profitable career is both an art and a science. While talent and creativity are crucial, achieving financial success requires strategic planning, diversified income streams, and a clear understanding of the writing industry. In today's world, writers have more opportunities than ever to monetize their skills, from traditional publishing to innovative digital platforms.

This chapter explores actionable strategies to help you transform your craft into a sustainable and lucrative career, empowering you to earn a living while pursuing your passion for storytelling.

The Mindset for Monetizing Writing

Before diving into strategies, cultivating the right mindset is essential:

1. See Yourself as an Entrepreneur

Writing is not just an art; it's a business. Treat your work as a product and yourself as a brand.

2. Embrace Value Creation

Monetizing your craft means delivering value to your audience. Whether through entertainment, education, or inspiration, your work should meet a need or solve a problem.

3. Stay Adaptable

The writing landscape is constantly evolving. Stay open to new opportunities and platforms that can expand your income streams.

Traditional Income Streams for Writers
1. Traditional Publishing
Publishing through established publishing houses remains a viable option for writers.
Steps to Succeed:

- Write a compelling query letter and synopsis to pitch your work to agents.
- Research publishers that align with your genre and style.
- Prepare for a slower income stream, as advances and royalties take time to materialize.

Advantages:

- Access to professional editing, marketing, and distribution networks.
- Credibility and prestige within the industry.

Challenges:

- High competition and limited control over creative and marketing decisions.

2. Self-Publishing
Self-publishing offers writers complete control over their work and higher royalty rates.
Steps to Succeed:

- Choose a platform like Amazon Kindle Direct Publishing (KDP), IngramSpark, or Draft2Digital.
- Invest in professional editing, cover design, and formatting.
- Use targeted marketing strategies, such as Amazon ads, email lists, and social media.

Advantages:

- Retain creative control and earn up to 70% royalties.
- Ability to publish on your timeline without gatekeepers.

Challenges:

- Upfront costs for production and marketing.
- Greater responsibility for reaching and engaging readers.

3. Freelance Writing

Freelance opportunities allow writers to earn steady income while honing their skills.

Types of Work:

- Articles and blog posts.
- Copywriting and content writing.
- Ghostwriting for books or speeches.

Steps to Succeed:

- Build a portfolio showcasing your best work.
- Use platforms like Upwork, Fiverr, or ProBlogger to find clients.
- Network with professionals and pitch directly to companies or publications.

Advantages:

- Flexible work arrangements and a variety of projects.
- Immediate income compared to long-term book royalties.

Challenges:

- Competitive rates and the need for ongoing client acquisition.

Innovative and Unique Income Streams

1. Digital Products

Create downloadable products that provide value to your audience.

Examples:

- Writing guides or workbooks.
- Templates for authors, such as query letter samples or character profiles.
- Printable planners for tracking word counts, deadlines, or story arcs.

Platforms:

- Sell on Etsy, Gumroad, or your own website.

Advantages:

- Passive income with minimal ongoing effort.
- High scalability with global reach.

2. Online Courses and Workshops

Leverage your expertise to teach others.

Examples:

- Create a course on outlining, self-publishing, or writing for specific genres.
- Host workshops on creative writing, storytelling techniques, or editing.

Platforms:

- Use platforms like Teachable, Udemy, or Skillshare to reach a broad audience.
- Offer live workshops through Zoom or in-person events.

Advantages:

- High earning potential with low upfront costs.
- Builds authority and grows your audience.

3. Subscription-Based Platforms

Offer exclusive content through membership services.

Examples:

- Publish serialized stories or bonus material on Patreon.
- Share behind-the-scenes content, writing tips, or early access to new work.

How to Succeed:

- Offer tiered rewards to cater to different audience budgets.
- Consistently engage with your subscribers to build loyalty.

Advantages:

- Reliable, recurring income.
- Builds a dedicated community around your work.

4. Merchandise and Licensing

Expand your income by turning your writing into tangible products.

Examples:

- Merchandise with quotes or themes from your work (e.g., mugs, T-shirts, journals).
- Licensing your stories for film, TV, or graphic novels.

Platforms:

- Use Print-on-Demand services like Redbubble or Society6.
- Approach agents or producers to pitch your work for adaptation.

Advantages:

- Diverse revenue streams beyond book sales.
- Increases brand visibility.

5. Affiliate Marketing

Earn commissions by recommending products or services to your audience.

Examples:

- Promote writing tools, software, or books.
- Include affiliate links in blogs, newsletters, or YouTube videos.

How to Succeed:

- Choose products aligned with your niche and audience's interests.
- Be transparent about affiliate relationships to build trust.

Advantages:

- Passive income with minimal effort.
- Requires no product creation or inventory.

6. Public Speaking and Consulting

Share your knowledge through speaking engagements or one-on-one services.

Examples:

- Deliver keynote speeches at writing conferences or literary festivals.
- Offer manuscript critiques, coaching, or strategy sessions for aspiring authors.

How to Succeed:

- Build a professional website showcasing your expertise and services.
- Network with event organizers and writing communities.

Advantages:

- High earning potential.
- Positions you as an industry expert.

Strategies for Scaling Your Writing Income
1. Build an Author Platform
Your platform is the foundation for all income streams.
Steps to Build a Platform:

- Create a professional website with a blog, contact form, and links to your work.
- Build an email list to engage directly with your audience.
- Use social media to showcase your personality and expertise.

2. Diversify Income Streams
Relying on a single source of income is risky. Combine multiple streams to create financial stability.
Examples:

- Pair book royalties with freelance writing and online courses.
- Combine Patreon memberships with merchandise sales and public speaking.

3. Leverage SEO and Content Marketing
Drive traffic to your website or books using search engine optimization (SEO) and high-quality content.
Examples:

- Write blog posts on writing tips, genre insights, or industry trends.
- Use keywords related to your niche to attract your target audience.

4. Collaborate with Other Creators
Partnerships can expand your reach and open new opportunities.
Examples:

- Co-author a book or contribute to an anthology.
- Host joint webinars or workshops with other writers.

Tips for Long-Term Success

1. **Invest in Yourself:** Attend writing workshops, conferences, and courses to refine your craft and expand your network.
2. **Stay Consistent:** Regularly produce and promote new content to maintain momentum.
3. **Adapt to Trends:** Keep an eye on industry changes and emerging platforms to stay ahead.
4. **Measure and Optimize:** Track your income streams and focus on the most profitable ones.

Conclusion: Turning Passion into Profit

Monetizing your craft requires creativity, perseverance, and strategic thinking. By exploring diverse income streams, building your platform, and consistently delivering value to your audience, you can transform writing from a passion into a highly profitable career.

Chapter 17: Passive Income for Authors

How to Create Systems That Make Money While You Sleep, Through eBooks, Courses, and More

One of the most powerful benefits of being an author in the digital age is the ability to generate passive income. Passive income allows you to earn money long after the initial effort of creating a product. By leveraging scalable systems and platforms, you can build a portfolio of income-generating assets that work for you 24/7.

This chapter explores proven strategies for creating passive income streams tailored for authors, from eBooks and online courses to digital products and affiliate marketing. You'll learn how to set up these systems, maximize their earning potential, and achieve financial freedom while focusing on your passion for writing.

What Is Passive Income?

Passive income is money earned with minimal ongoing effort after the initial setup. For authors, it involves creating assets—like books, courses, or digital downloads—that can be sold repeatedly without requiring additional production work.

Active Income vs. Passive Income

- **Active Income:** Requires continuous effort, such as freelance writing or live coaching.
- **Passive Income:** Earned from pre-created products or systems, like royalties from an eBook.

Why Passive Income Matters for Authors

1. **Financial Stability:** Provides consistent income, reducing reliance on sporadic book advances or freelance projects.
2. **Freedom to Create:** Allows you to focus on new creative endeavors without financial pressure.
3. **Scalability:** Digital products and systems can reach a global audience, multiplying your earnings without increasing your workload.
4. **Sustainability:** Generates income even during breaks, ensuring long-term career viability.

Step 1: Building Passive Income Systems

Passive income doesn't happen by chance—it requires deliberate planning and execution. Here's how to get started:

1. Identify Your Strengths and Niche

Choose a niche or area of expertise that aligns with your writing and audience's needs.

Examples:

- A romance author could create a series of eBooks on "Writing Heartfelt Love Stories."
- A nonfiction writer could develop a course on "How to Self-Publish on a Budget."

Why It Matters:

Focusing on your niche ensures you attract the right audience and build credibility.

2. Choose the Right Platforms

Leverage platforms designed for passive income generation.

Options for Authors:

- **Amazon KDP:** Self-publish eBooks and earn royalties on every sale.
- **Gumroad/Payhip:** Sell digital products like guides, templates, or workbooks.
- **Teachable/Udemy:** Host and sell online courses.
- **Patreon:** Offer exclusive content to subscribers.

Why It Matters:

Choosing the right platform streamlines distribution and ensures your products reach a wide audience.

Step 2: Creating High-Value Products
1. Self-Published eBooks
Self-publishing is one of the most accessible ways to generate passive income.
How to Succeed:

- Write a series of eBooks to maximize sales potential.
- Use a professional cover design and formatting to increase credibility.
- Optimize your book's description and keywords for Amazon search visibility.

Example Income Potential:
A well-marketed eBook priced at $4.99 can earn $3.49 in royalties per sale. Selling just 100 copies per month generates $349 in passive income.

2. Online Courses
Turn your expertise into an educational product.
Examples of Courses:

- "Worldbuilding for Fantasy Writers."
- "How to Write a Bestseller in 90 Days."

How to Create a Course:

- Outline your course into clear, actionable modules.
- Record videos, create worksheets, and include quizzes for engagement.
- Use platforms like Teachable or Thinkific to host your course.

Advantages:
Courses often have higher price points ($50–$500), resulting in significant earnings from fewer sales.

3. Digital Products
Digital products are one-time creations that can be sold repeatedly.
Examples:

- Writing prompts or story ideas collections.
- Templates for book outlines, character development, or marketing plans.
- Printable journals, planners, or writing trackers.

How to Succeed:

- Focus on products that solve a problem or add value for your audience.

- Use marketplaces like Etsy, Gumroad, or your own website for distribution.

4. Audiobooks
Convert your books into audiobooks to reach a new audience and diversify income.
How to Succeed:

- Use platforms like ACX or Findaway Voices to produce and distribute audiobooks.
- Hire a professional narrator or record your own if you have the skills and equipment.

Why It Matters:
The audiobook market is growing rapidly, providing additional revenue streams for existing content.

5. Memberships and Subscriptions
Create a recurring income model through exclusive content.
Ideas for Membership Content:

- Monthly short stories or serialized novels.
- Exclusive writing tips, Q&A sessions, or live webinars.
- Early access to your books or behind-the-scenes updates.

Platforms to Use:

- Patreon, Substack, or Ko-fi for recurring memberships.

Advantages:
Subscription models provide predictable monthly income.

Step 3: Marketing Your Passive Income Products

Creating products is only half the battle—you also need to market them effectively.

1. Build an Email List

An email list is one of the most reliable ways to promote your products.

How to Grow Your List:

- Offer a freebie, like a guide or short story, in exchange for email signups.
- Use email platforms like Mailchimp or ConvertKit to manage your list.

2. Leverage Social Media

Use platforms like Instagram, Twitter, and TikTok to showcase your work.

Content Ideas:

- Share snippets of your eBook or course.
- Post testimonials or success stories from customers.
- Engage with your audience by answering questions or hosting live sessions.

3. Optimize for SEO

Ensure your products are easy to find online.

Tips for SEO:

- Use relevant keywords in product titles, descriptions, and tags.
- Write blog posts related to your product topics and link to your sales page.

Step 4: Scaling Your Passive Income Streams

Once your systems are in place, focus on scaling to maximize earnings.

1. Diversify Your Portfolio

Offer a mix of eBooks, courses, and digital products to reach different segments of your audience.

2. Create Bundles

Combine related products into bundles at a discounted price to increase sales volume.

3. Use Paid Advertising

Invest in targeted ads on platforms like Amazon, Facebook, or Instagram to reach a broader audience.

4. Leverage Affiliate Marketing

Encourage others to promote your products in exchange for a commission.

How to Succeed:

- Create an affiliate program for your course or eBooks.
- Partner with bloggers, influencers, or fellow authors in your niche.

The Long-Term Benefits of Passive Income

1. **Financial Freedom:** Reduce reliance on active income and build a sustainable revenue stream.
2. **Scalability:** Passive products can reach a global audience without additional work.
3. **Time Flexibility:** Free up time to focus on writing, learning, or personal growth.

Conclusion: Building Your Passive Income Empire

Creating passive income systems as an author requires effort upfront, but the rewards are immense. By leveraging your skills, creativity, and available platforms, you can generate sustainable income that supports your writing career and lifestyle.

Chapter 18: Financial Planning for Writers
Practical Financial Management Tailored for Creatives and Authors

A thriving writing career is about more than crafting compelling stories—it requires sound financial planning. As a writer, your income can be unpredictable, fluctuating with book sales, freelance projects, or royalties. Learning how to manage your finances effectively ensures stability, reduces stress, and allows you to focus on your creative work.

This chapter explores essential financial strategies tailored specifically for authors and creatives. From budgeting and saving to navigating taxes and diversifying income, you'll gain the tools needed to build a secure financial foundation and sustain your writing career for the long term.

Why Financial Planning Is Essential for Writers

1. **Income Fluctuations:** Writing income is often irregular. Planning ensures you can weather slow periods without financial strain.
2. **Career Longevity:** Financial stability allows you to focus on writing instead of chasing quick-paying, non-creative work.
3. **Freedom to Create:** A solid financial base gives you the freedom to take creative risks or invest in passion projects.

Step 1: Understand Your Income Sources

Writers often earn from multiple streams, including:

- Book royalties.
- Advances from publishers.
- Freelance writing projects.
- Speaking engagements or workshops.
- Digital products like eBooks, courses, or templates.

Action Steps:

- List all your income sources and calculate their average contribution to your monthly earnings.
- Identify your most consistent and lucrative streams to prioritize and grow.

Step 2: Budgeting for Writers

A well-structured budget is the foundation of financial planning.

1. Track Your Expenses

Understanding where your money goes helps you manage it effectively.

Tools to Use:

- Apps like Mint, YNAB (You Need a Budget), or PocketGuard.
- A simple spreadsheet to categorize expenses.

Categories to Track:

- Essentials: Rent/mortgage, utilities, groceries.
- Career Expenses: Software subscriptions, marketing, website hosting.
- Variable Expenses: Travel, dining out, entertainment.

2. Create a Monthly Budget

Design a budget tailored to your irregular income.

Steps:

- Calculate your average monthly income based on the past 6–12 months.
- Allocate 50% of income to needs, 30% to wants, and 20% to savings/debt repayment (adjust as needed).
- Include a category for reinvesting in your writing career, such as editing services or advertising.

3. Plan for Lean Months

Irregular income requires preparation for slow periods.

How to Build a Cushion:

- Save 3–6 months of living expenses in an emergency fund.
- During high-earning months, allocate extra income toward savings or debt.

Step 3: Manage Taxes as a Writer

Taxes can be complex for writers, especially those with multiple income streams or self-employment status.

1. Track Your Income and Expenses

Keep detailed records of your earnings and career-related expenses.

Deductible Expenses for Writers:

- Office supplies and equipment.
- Writing software and subscriptions.
- Travel expenses for research or events.
- Marketing and advertising costs.
- Home office expenses (if applicable).

Tools to Use:

- QuickBooks Self-Employed, FreshBooks, or Wave for expense tracking.

2. Estimate Quarterly Taxes

If you're self-employed, you may need to pay estimated taxes quarterly.

How to Calculate:

- Use IRS Form 1040-ES to estimate your tax liability.
- Set aside 20–30% of your income for taxes in a separate account.

3. Hire a Professional

A tax professional or accountant familiar with creative industries can help you maximize deductions and navigate complex tax laws.

Step 4: Build a Savings Strategy
Saving is critical for long-term financial stability and unexpected expenses.
1. Emergency Fund
An emergency fund provides a safety net for lean months or unforeseen costs.
Goal: Save 3–6 months' worth of essential expenses.
2. Retirement Savings
Freelancers and self-employed writers need to plan for retirement independently.
Options:

- **Traditional or Roth IRA:** Tax-advantaged accounts for individual retirement savings.
- **Solo 401(k):** Ideal for self-employed individuals with higher contribution limits.
- **SEP IRA:** Simplified Employee Pension plan for freelancers.

3. Project-Based Savings
Set aside money for future career investments, such as professional editing, marketing campaigns, or writing retreats.

Step 5: Diversify Your Income
Relying on a single income source is risky. Diversifying income streams ensures financial stability.
Ideas for Diversification:

- **Freelance Writing:** Articles, blogs, or ghostwriting projects.
- **Courses and Workshops:** Teach writing or other skills online or in-person.
- **Digital Products:** Templates, guides, or planners for other writers.
- **Affiliate Marketing:** Promote products or services relevant to your audience.
- **Public Speaking:** Offer talks at schools, conferences, or literary events.

Step 6: Reduce Financial Stress
Managing finances effectively reduces stress and allows you to focus on your creative work.
1. Automate Savings and Bills

- Use automatic transfers to savings accounts and schedule bill payments to avoid late fees.

2. Simplify Your Finances

- Consolidate accounts and streamline your financial tools to reduce complexity.

3. Seek Financial Education

- Read books like *The Money Book for Freelancers* by Joseph D'Agnese and Denise Kiernan.
- Take online courses on financial management tailored to creatives.

Step 7: Reinvest in Your Writing Career
Reinvesting part of your income into your career is essential for growth.
Smart Investments for Writers:

- **Professional Development:** Attend workshops or hire a writing coach.
- **Marketing:** Allocate funds for ads, social media campaigns, or book launches.
- **Equipment:** Upgrade to a better laptop or ergonomic workspace.

Step 8: Long-Term Financial Planning
1. Set Financial Goals
Define short-term, mid-term, and long-term financial objectives.
Examples:

- Short-term: Save for a conference or retreat.
- Mid-term: Pay off debt or fund a book launch.
- Long-term: Achieve a stable income through passive streams.

2. Create a Business Plan
If writing is your career, treat it like a business.
Include:

- Revenue goals.
- Expense management strategies.
- Marketing and growth plans.

Common Financial Mistakes to Avoid

1. **Inconsistent Record-Keeping:** Leads to missed deductions and budgeting errors.
2. **Overinvesting:** Spending too much upfront without ensuring a return on investment.
3. **Ignoring Retirement Savings:** Leads to financial insecurity later in life.
4. **Underestimating Taxes:** Can result in unexpected liabilities and penalties.

Conclusion: Financial Empowerment for Writers

Financial planning is not just about managing money—it's about creating a foundation that allows you to thrive creatively and professionally. By implementing the strategies in this chapter, you can take control of your finances, reduce stress, and focus on building a sustainable and rewarding writing career.

Chapter 19: Crowdfunding Creativity
Leveraging Platforms Like Kickstarter to Fund Your Writing Projects

Crowdfunding has revolutionized the way creators bring their projects to life. For writers, platforms like Kickstarter, Indiegogo, and Patreon provide the opportunity to raise funds directly from fans and supporters, bypassing traditional publishing gatekeepers. Crowdfunding not only provides financial support but also helps you build a dedicated community around your work, creating a network of readers who are invested in your success.

This chapter explores the strategies and steps necessary to run a successful crowdfunding campaign for your writing projects, from concept to execution. You'll learn how to craft compelling pitches, engage your audience, and use crowdfunding as a launchpad for your creative career.

The Benefits of Crowdfunding for Writers

1. **Access to Funds:** Secure financial support to cover editing, design, printing, marketing, or living expenses while writing.
2. **Creative Freedom:** Retain full creative control over your project without relying on traditional publishers.
3. **Audience Engagement:** Build a loyal community of readers who are emotionally and financially invested in your success.
4. **Market Validation:** Gauge interest in your project before committing to production, reducing financial risk.

Step 1: Choosing the Right Crowdfunding Platform
Different platforms cater to different needs. Select the one that aligns with your goals.

1. Kickstarter

- Best for project-based funding with a clear goal and timeline.
- Operates on an "all-or-nothing" model—you only receive funds if your campaign meets its goal.
- Ideal for funding book launches, special editions, or new series.

2. Indiegogo

- Offers both fixed funding (like Kickstarter) and flexible funding (keep funds raised, even if the goal isn't met).
- Suitable for writers needing flexible goals or ongoing support.

3. Patreon

- A subscription-based model for ongoing support from fans.
- Ideal for writers creating serialized content, such as monthly chapters, short stories, or behind-the-scenes updates.

Pro Tip: Research successful campaigns on each platform in your genre to determine the best fit for your project.

Step 2: Planning Your Crowdfunding Campaign

1. Define Your Goal
Set a clear, realistic funding target based on your project's needs.

Factors to Consider:

- Costs for editing, cover design, formatting, and printing.
- Marketing and distribution expenses.
- Fees for the platform (typically 5–8% of total funds raised).

Example Budget Breakdown:

- Editing: $1,500
- Cover Design: $500
- Printing Costs: $2,000
- Marketing: $1,000
  Total Goal: $5,000

2. Develop a Strong Concept
Your project should have a clear and compelling premise that excites potential backers.

How to Refine Your Concept:

- Identify your target audience. Who will love this book?
- Highlight what makes your project unique.
- Focus on benefits for your backers, such as exclusive rewards or involvement in the creative process.

Example Concept:
"I'm creating a fantasy novel that reimagines ancient myths with a modern twist, featuring a diverse cast of characters. This crowdfunding campaign will help fund professional editing, cover design, and a limited-edition hardcover release."

3. Craft a Detailed Timeline
Backers want to know when they can expect results. Outline key milestones for your project.

Sample Timeline:

- Campaign Launch: January 1
- Campaign End: February 15
- Editing Completed: March 30
- Printing: April 15
- Book Delivery: May 15

Step 3: Creating a Compelling Campaign Page
Your campaign page is your pitch. Make it engaging, professional, and visually appealing.
1. Write a Persuasive Pitch

- Start with a hook that grabs attention.
- Explain why your project matters and what sets it apart.
- Share your passion and vision to build emotional connection.
- End with a strong call to action, inviting people to back your project.

Example Opening:
"Imagine a world where forgotten myths come alive in a battle for survival. *The Forgotten Pantheon* is a thrilling fantasy novel that combines ancient legends with gripping storytelling—and I need your help to bring it to life."

2. Use Visuals and Videos

- Create a professional-quality video explaining your project and its importance. Keep it under 3 minutes.
- Include images, mockups of book covers, and progress updates.

3. Offer Irresistible Rewards
Backers need incentives to support your campaign.
Ideas for Reward Tiers:

- $5: Digital thank-you and name in acknowledgments.
- $15: eBook copy of the book.
- $25: Signed paperback copy.
- $50: Limited-edition hardcover and exclusive bookmark.
- $100: Personalized thank-you note and a writing workshop invitation.

Tips:

- Ensure reward tiers are affordable and manageable to produce.
- Offer exclusive, limited-edition rewards to create urgency.

Step 4: Promoting Your Campaign
A successful crowdfunding campaign requires strategic promotion.
1. Build Anticipation Before Launch

- Share teasers on social media, such as snippets from your book or behind-the-scenes photos.
- Announce your campaign launch date and invite followers to join your email list for updates.

2. Leverage Your Network

- Reach out to friends, family, and colleagues to support your campaign early on.
- Ask them to share your campaign with their networks.

3. Use Social Media Strategically

- Create engaging posts about your project, including videos, visuals, and testimonials.
- Use relevant hashtags to reach your target audience.
- Host live Q&A sessions or behind-the-scenes updates.

4. Engage with Your Backers

- Thank supporters publicly to show appreciation.
- Provide regular updates on your campaign's progress.

Step 5: Running Your Campaign
1. Monitor Progress Daily

- Track your campaign's performance and identify which strategies are driving the most backers.
- Adjust your marketing efforts if needed to maintain momentum.

2. Keep the Excitement Alive

- Announce milestones, such as reaching 50% of your goal.
- Introduce stretch goals for additional funding (e.g., "If we reach $6,000, I'll add a bonus chapter or exclusive artwork!").

3. Stay Responsive

- Answer questions and comments promptly to build trust and engagement.

Step 6: Delivering on Your Promises
A successful campaign doesn't end when it's funded—it's fulfilled when backers receive what you promised.

1. Stay Transparent

- Keep backers informed about progress, delays, or changes.
- Share photos or videos of your work in progress.

2. Deliver Rewards on Time

- Create a detailed fulfillment plan, including shipping and digital delivery.
- Use platforms like BackerKit for reward management.

3. Express Gratitude

- Thank your backers personally, either through notes, emails, or acknowledgments in your book.
- Share the impact of their support, such as photos of the final product or testimonials from readers.

Success Stories: Inspiration from Writers

1. *The Way of Kings Leatherbound Edition* **by Brandon Sanderson**

- Raised $6.7 million on Kickstarter.
- Offered limited-edition, beautifully bound copies of a beloved fantasy novel.

2. *Empowered* **by Cat Lantigua**

- Raised $12,000 on Kickstarter to fund a book about inspiring young women.
- Focused on a clear mission and engaged a supportive community.

Common Crowdfunding Mistakes to Avoid

1. **Unrealistic Goals:** Set a target that reflects your actual needs and audience size.
2. **Poor Planning:** Lack of preparation can lead to missed deadlines and dissatisfied backers.
3. **Overpromising:** Offer rewards you can realistically deliver within your budget and timeline.

Conclusion: Crowdfunding as a Catalyst

Crowdfunding is more than a way to fund your writing projects—it's a tool to build your audience, showcase your creativity, and establish your brand. By following the strategies in this chapter, you can launch a successful campaign that not only finances your work but also connects you with readers who believe in your vision.

Chapter 20: Publishing Profits

Maximizing Earnings Through Self-Publishing, Traditional Publishing, and Hybrid Approaches

In the rapidly evolving world of publishing, authors have more options than ever to bring their stories to readers and earn a living from their work. Each path—self-publishing, traditional publishing, and hybrid models—offers unique opportunities and challenges. To maximize your earnings as an author, it's essential to understand these avenues, leverage their strengths, and tailor your approach to your goals.

This chapter provides an in-depth guide to monetizing your work across publishing models, offering strategies to maximize profits and build a sustainable writing career.

Understanding the Publishing Models

1. Self-Publishing

In self-publishing, authors take full control of the publishing process, including writing, editing, design, and marketing.

Key Features:

- You retain all creative control and rights.
- Higher royalty rates (up to 70%) compared to traditional publishing.
- Requires upfront investment for production and marketing.

Best For:

- Authors with niche audiences.
- Writers who want full control over their work.
- Those willing to manage the business side of publishing.

2. Traditional Publishing

In traditional publishing, a publishing house handles the production, distribution, and marketing of your book in exchange for rights and a percentage of sales.

Key Features:

- Access to professional editors, designers, and marketers.
- Advance payments and royalties.
- Limited creative and financial control.

Best For:

- Writers aiming for wide distribution and credibility.
- Those who prefer a hands-off approach to publishing logistics.

3. Hybrid Publishing

Hybrid publishing combines aspects of self-publishing and traditional publishing, often requiring an upfront investment from the author while providing professional services.

Key Features:

- Authors retain more control than traditional publishing.
- Professional production and marketing services are provided.
- Royalties are often higher than traditional publishing but lower than self-publishing.

Best For:

- Authors with the budget to invest in publishing but lacking the time or expertise to handle it themselves.
- Those seeking professional polish while maintaining some control.

Step 1: Maximizing Profits in Self-Publishing

Self-publishing can be highly profitable when done strategically.

1. Choose the Right Platform

- **Amazon Kindle Direct Publishing (KDP):** Dominates the eBook market; offers up to 70% royalties.
- **IngramSpark:** Ideal for print-on-demand books with wide distribution to bookstores and libraries.
- **Smashwords or Draft2Digital:** Distribute to multiple platforms, including Apple Books, Barnes & Noble, and Kobo.

Pro Tip: Use multiple platforms to maximize reach and earnings.

2. Invest in Quality Production

Readers judge books by their covers and quality.

Essential Investments:

- **Professional Editing:** Ensures your book is polished and error-free.
- **Cover Design:** Attracts readers and conveys genre.
- **Formatting:** For both eBook and print versions to ensure readability.

3. Price Strategically

Pricing can significantly impact sales volume and profits.

Strategies:

- Start with lower prices ($0.99–$2.99) for eBooks to attract readers and build an audience.
- Use tiered pricing, increasing the price after building reviews and demand.

- Offer free or discounted promotions to boost visibility and rankings.

4. Leverage Amazon KDP Select
Enroll your eBook in KDP Select for exclusive benefits:

- Access to Kindle Unlimited (KU) readers and payment per page read.
- Opportunities for free or discounted promotions.

Caution: KDP Select requires exclusivity, meaning you can't sell your eBook on other platforms.

5. Build a Backlist
Publishing multiple books increases earnings by giving readers more to buy.

How to Succeed:

- Write series or related books to encourage binge reading.
- Bundle older books into box sets for additional revenue streams.

Step 2: Maximizing Profits in Traditional Publishing
Traditional publishing offers stability and prestige but requires careful navigation to maximize earnings.

1. Negotiate Your Contract
Advances and royalties vary widely. Work with an agent to negotiate favorable terms.

Key Points to Negotiate:

- Higher royalties for print (10–15%) and eBooks (25–40%).
- Retention of subsidiary rights (e.g., film, TV, audiobooks) to maximize additional revenue.
- Clauses for reversion of rights if the book goes out of print.

2. Leverage Your Advance
While advances are paid upfront, they are often split into installments. Use this money wisely:

- Cover writing-related expenses (e.g., research, software).
- Invest in personal marketing efforts to supplement the publisher's efforts.

3. Promote Your Book Independently
Publishers often have limited marketing budgets for new authors. Take initiative to boost your book's visibility.

Strategies:

- Build your author platform through social media, email lists, and a professional website.
- Schedule book signings, blog tours, or interviews to reach new readers.

Step 3: Maximizing Profits with Hybrid Publishing

Hybrid publishing provides a middle ground, combining professional services with author control.

1. Research Reputable Hybrid Publishers

Not all hybrid publishers are created equal. Look for companies with:

- Transparent pricing and royalty structures.
- Proven success stories and satisfied authors.
- Clear contracts outlining responsibilities and rights.

2. Calculate ROI

Hybrid publishing often requires significant upfront costs. Ensure potential earnings justify the investment.

Break-Even Analysis:

- Compare total production costs to expected royalties.
- Estimate sales volume needed to recover your investment.

Step 4: General Strategies to Boost Publishing Profits

Regardless of your publishing path, these strategies can enhance your earnings.

1. Diversify Your Formats

Offer your book in multiple formats to reach different audiences.

Examples:

- **eBooks:** For digital readers and global reach.
- **Print Books:** For libraries, bookstores, and collectors.
- **Audiobooks:** For commuters and audiobook enthusiasts.

2. Expand Your Revenue Streams

Supplement book sales with additional income sources.

Ideas:

- Host workshops or webinars related to your book's topic.
- Create merchandise, such as T-shirts, mugs, or posters featuring your book's themes or quotes.
- License your work for adaptations, such as film, TV, or graphic novels.

3. Optimize Marketing Efforts

Invest time and resources into effective book promotion.

Strategies:

- **Email Marketing:** Build and nurture an email list to announce new releases and promotions.
- **Social Media Advertising:** Use targeted ads on Facebook, Instagram, or Amazon to reach your ideal readers.
- **Collaborate with Influencers:** Partner with book bloggers, reviewers, or influencers in your genre.

4. Build a Long-Term Career Strategy
Publishing profits grow over time as you build your brand and backlist.
Steps to Take:

- Establish consistent writing and publishing schedules.
- Diversify your portfolio by exploring different genres or formats.
- Foster relationships with readers through newsletters and fan communities.

Common Mistakes to Avoid

1. **Neglecting Quality:** Cutting corners on editing or design can harm your reputation and sales.
2. **Overpricing:** High prices may deter readers, especially for new authors.
3. **Ignoring Marketing:** Even the best book won't sell without visibility.
4. **Failing to Plan for Taxes:** Set aside a portion of your earnings to cover taxes, especially if self-publishing.

Conclusion: Choosing Your Path to Publishing Profits
Maximizing publishing profits requires a strategic approach tailored to your goals, audience, and resources. Whether you choose self-publishing, traditional publishing, or a hybrid model, understanding the mechanics of each path empowers you to make informed decisions and build a profitable writing career.

Part V: The Ultimate Life Balance

Chapter 21: Burnout-Proof Writing
Techniques to Avoid Burnout, Sustain Energy, and Enjoy the Process of Creation

Burnout is a silent killer of creativity. It creeps in when deadlines loom, when self-imposed pressure mounts, or when the joy of writing fades under the weight of endless to-do lists. For writers, burnout can lead to prolonged creative blocks, stress, and even the decision to abandon projects altogether.

The key to a sustainable and fulfilling writing career is learning how to recognize, prevent, and recover from burnout. This chapter explores practical techniques to help you maintain energy, rekindle your passion, and enjoy the process of creation for years to come.

What Is Burnout?

Burnout is a state of physical, mental, and emotional exhaustion caused by prolonged stress or overwork. For writers, it manifests as:

- **Creative fatigue:** Difficulty generating ideas or completing projects.
- **Procrastination:** Avoiding writing due to feelings of overwhelm or apathy.
- **Self-doubt:** A persistent belief that your work isn't good enough.
- **Physical symptoms:** Fatigue, headaches, or difficulty sleeping.

The Causes of Writer Burnout

1. Unrealistic Expectations

Setting unattainable goals, like finishing a novel in a week or writing 10,000 words a day, creates unnecessary stress.

2. Overcommitment

Juggling multiple projects, deadlines, or responsibilities can quickly lead to exhaustion.

3. Lack of Balance

Focusing exclusively on writing at the expense of rest, hobbies, and relationships disrupts well-being.

4. Perfectionism

Obsessing over flawless work slows progress and increases frustration.

5. Neglecting Self-Care

Skipping meals, sleep, or exercise to "make time" for writing diminishes energy and creativity.

Step 1: Recognizing Burnout Early

Preventing burnout begins with awareness. Look for these warning signs:

- **Loss of motivation:** Writing feels like a chore instead of a passion.
- **Inconsistent productivity:** You alternate between overworking and avoiding writing altogether.
- **Emotional distress:** You feel irritable, anxious, or detached from your work.
- **Physical symptoms:** Fatigue, tension, or frequent illnesses.

Action Step: Reflect on your current habits and identify areas where stress or exhaustion may be building.

Step 2: Techniques to Avoid Burnout

1. Set Realistic Goals

Ambition is important, but setting achievable targets prevents overwhelm.

How to Set Realistic Goals:

- Break large projects into smaller, manageable tasks (e.g., writing 500 words daily instead of completing a chapter).
- Use SMART goals (Specific, Measurable, Achievable, Relevant, Time-bound) to create clarity.
- Celebrate small wins to stay motivated and maintain momentum.

2. Prioritize Rest and Recovery

Rest is as essential to creativity as writing itself.

How to Rest Effectively:

- **Sleep:** Aim for 7–9 hours per night to recharge your body and mind.
- **Breaks:** Follow the Pomodoro Technique (25 minutes of focus, 5 minutes of rest) or take longer breaks after deep work sessions.
- **Day Off:** Dedicate at least one day per week to non-writing activities.

3. Practice Mindful Writing

Mindfulness helps you focus on the joy of writing rather than external pressures.

How to Practice Mindful Writing:

- Begin each session with deep breathing or meditation to center yourself.
- Write without judgment—focus on flow rather than perfection.
- Reflect on what excites you about your story or project.

4. Embrace Balance

Integrating writing into a balanced lifestyle prevents it from becoming overwhelming.

Strategies for Balance:

- Schedule time for hobbies, exercise, and socializing alongside writing.
- Create boundaries around your writing time to protect personal and family time.
- Limit overwork by setting daily writing time caps, such as two focused hours.

5. Manage External Pressures
External demands can add to burnout if left unchecked.
How to Manage Pressures:

- Communicate realistic deadlines with editors, agents, or collaborators.
- Say no to projects that don't align with your goals or capacity.
- Delegate tasks (e.g., hire a virtual assistant for marketing or administrative work).

6. Build a Support System
A network of supportive peers and mentors can help you navigate challenges.
How to Build Support:

- Join writing groups or online communities for encouragement and accountability.
- Share your struggles with trusted friends or family members.
- Seek professional advice, such as therapy or coaching, if needed.

Step 3: Sustaining Energy for the Long Term
1. Create a Writing Ritual
A consistent routine reduces decision fatigue and fosters focus.
Ideas for Writing Rituals:

- Begin with a cup of tea, a short meditation, or journaling.
- Use a designated writing space to signal your brain it's time to work.
- End each session with a brief review or gratitude practice.

2. Fuel Your Body and Mind
Good nutrition, hydration, and movement are essential for sustained energy.
Tips for Physical Wellness:

- Eat brain-boosting foods like fruits, vegetables, nuts, and whole grains.
- Stay hydrated with water or herbal teas.

- Incorporate regular physical activity, such as yoga, walking, or stretching.

3. Stay Inspired
Reignite your passion by seeking inspiration outside of writing.
Sources of Inspiration:

- Read books in your genre or explore new ones.
- Watch films, attend art exhibits, or explore nature for fresh perspectives.
- Engage in creative hobbies like painting, music, or cooking.

4. Focus on Your "Why"
Reconnect with the reasons you write.
Questions to Reflect On:

- Why does this story matter to me?
- What do I hope readers will feel or learn from my work?
- How does writing enrich my life?

Step 4: Recovering from Burnout
If burnout has already set in, recovery is possible with patience and care.

1. Take a Break
Step away from writing for a few days or weeks to recharge.
How to Use Breaks Wisely:

- Engage in restorative activities, such as hiking, journaling, or spending time with loved ones.
- Reflect on what led to burnout and how you can adjust your habits.

2. Revisit Your Creative Process
Simplify or refresh your approach to writing.
Ideas to Revitalize Creativity:

- Experiment with a new genre, style, or format.
- Set aside perfectionism and write just for fun.
- Revisit unfinished projects or ideas that excite you.

3. Seek Professional Help
If burnout persists, consider working with a therapist or coach to address underlying stressors and develop sustainable habits.

Step 5: Enjoying the Process of Creation
Writing should be a fulfilling and joyful experience.
1. Celebrate Progress, Not Perfection
Focus on growth rather than comparing yourself to others or striving for unattainable standards.
How to Celebrate Progress:

- Reflect on how your skills and confidence have grown over time.
- Acknowledge small milestones, like finishing a draft or receiving positive feedback.

2. Infuse Playfulness into Writing
Reignite your passion by rediscovering the fun in storytelling.
Ideas:

- Write a silly short story or experiment with absurd prompts.
- Collaborate with a friend on a playful writing challenge.
- Turn off the inner critic and write freely without worrying about the end result.

Conclusion: Writing Without Burnout

Burnout doesn't have to define your writing journey. By setting realistic goals, maintaining balance, and embracing the joy of creation, you can sustain your energy and passion for the long haul. Writing is a marathon, not a sprint, and the techniques in this chapter will help you pace yourself while savoring every step.

Chapter 22: Health and Creativity
How Physical and Mental Well-Being Fuel Long-Term Creativity

Creativity thrives in a healthy body and mind. Writing, though often perceived as a sedentary and cerebral activity, requires sustained physical energy, emotional resilience, and mental clarity. Overlooking your health can lead to fatigue, creative blocks, and burnout, limiting your ability to produce your best work.

This chapter explores the profound connection between physical and mental well-being and long-term creativity. You'll discover actionable strategies to nurture your health, boost your creative output, and sustain your passion for writing over the long haul.

The Connection Between Health and Creativity

1. **Brain-Body Link:** A healthy body supports optimal brain function, including memory, focus, and idea generation.
2. **Emotional Resilience:** Mental well-being enhances your ability to handle setbacks, self-doubt, and stress, all common challenges for writers.
3. **Energy Reserves:** Physical fitness provides the stamina needed for long writing sessions or deadlines.
4. **Creative Flow:** Balanced physical and mental health fosters the flow state where creativity flourishes.

Step 1: Physical Health for Writers
1. Nutrition for Creativity

The food you eat fuels your brain, directly influencing your ability to think clearly and create effectively.

Brain-Boosting Foods:

- **Leafy Greens:** Spinach, kale, and broccoli support cognitive health.
- **Omega-3 Fatty Acids:** Found in salmon, walnuts, and flaxseeds, these improve memory and focus.
- **Whole Grains:** Brown rice, quinoa, and oatmeal provide sustained energy.
- **Antioxidant-Rich Foods:** Berries, dark chocolate, and green tea protect brain cells from oxidative stress.

Tips for Writers:

- Avoid heavy, processed meals that cause energy crashes.
- Stay hydrated; even mild dehydration can impair concentration.
- Keep healthy snacks on hand, such as nuts, fruits, or yogurt, for sustained energy during writing sessions.

2. Physical Activity for Sustained Energy

Regular exercise boosts energy levels, improves mood, and enhances cognitive function.

Recommended Activities for Writers:

- **Cardio:** Walking, jogging, or cycling increases blood flow to the brain, improving creativity and problem-solving.
- **Strength Training:** Builds endurance for long periods of sitting and helps maintain posture.
- **Stretching or Yoga:** Relieves tension in the neck, shoulders, and back caused by desk work.

Action Steps:

- Incorporate short movement breaks into your writing routine.
- Use the Pomodoro Technique to alternate 25 minutes of focused work with 5 minutes of stretching.
- Aim for at least 30 minutes of moderate exercise most days.

3. Ergonomics for Writers

A poorly set-up workspace can lead to physical discomfort, reducing your ability to focus and write.

Optimize Your Workspace:

- **Chair:** Invest in an ergonomic chair with lumbar support.
- **Desk:** Adjust the height so your elbows are at a 90-degree angle while typing.
- **Screen Position:** Place your monitor at eye level to avoid neck strain.
- **Lighting:** Use natural or warm lighting to reduce eye strain.

Tips for Avoiding Pain:

- Take frequent breaks to stretch and reset your posture.
- Use a standing desk or alternate between sitting and standing.
- Practice wrist exercises to prevent repetitive strain injuries.

Step 2: Mental Health for Creativity
1. Cultivate Emotional Resilience
Writing can be emotionally taxing, especially when dealing with rejection, self-doubt, or creative blocks.
Strategies for Resilience:

- **Reframe Rejection:** View setbacks as opportunities to learn and grow.
- **Develop a Support System:** Share your journey with trusted friends, mentors, or writing groups.
- **Celebrate Small Wins:** Acknowledge progress to build confidence and motivation.

2. Manage Stress
Chronic stress impairs memory, focus, and creative thinking.
Stress-Reduction Techniques:

- **Mindfulness Meditation:** Spend 5–10 minutes daily focusing on your breath to calm your mind.
- **Journaling:** Write about your thoughts and feelings to process emotions and gain clarity.
- **Time Management:** Use tools like calendars, to-do lists, or project management apps to reduce overwhelm.

3. Sleep for Creativity
Sleep is essential for cognitive function and creative problem-solving.
Tips for Better Sleep:

- **Establish a Routine:** Go to bed and wake up at the same time daily.
- **Limit Screen Time:** Avoid screens 1–2 hours before bedtime to promote melatonin production.
- **Create a Restful Environment:** Keep your bedroom cool, dark, and quiet.

Fun Fact: Many creative breakthroughs occur during sleep or in the moments between wakefulness and sleep.

4. Seek Professional Support When Needed
If you're struggling with anxiety, depression, or other mental health challenges, seeking help is a sign of strength.
Resources:

- Therapy or counseling for guidance and support.
- Writing-focused support groups to connect with peers who understand your challenges.

Step 3: Creative Habits That Enhance Well-Being

1. Practice Gratitude

Gratitude fosters positivity and shifts focus away from stress or self-doubt.

How to Practice:

- Keep a gratitude journal, noting 3 things you're thankful for daily.
- Reflect on the progress you've made in your writing journey.

2. Embrace Playfulness

Incorporating play into your routine nurtures creativity and prevents burnout.

Ideas:

- Experiment with new genres or styles.
- Write for fun without worrying about perfection or outcomes.
- Try creative prompts or collaborative storytelling.

3. Find Inspiration in Movement

Physical activity often sparks creativity.

How to Harness This:

- Take a walk and let your mind wander.
- Try writing outdoors or in new environments to refresh your perspective.

4. Schedule Downtime

Restorative activities recharge your mind and keep creativity flowing.

Suggestions:

- Read for pleasure to stimulate new ideas.
- Explore other art forms, such as painting, music, or photography.
- Spend time in nature to reduce stress and spark inspiration.

Step 4: Building a Sustainable Creative Life
1. Create a Balanced Routine
Balance writing with rest, exercise, and social activities to sustain long-term creativity.
Sample Daily Routine:

- Morning: Stretch or meditate, then write for a focused hour.
- Afternoon: Engage in physical activity, such as a walk or yoga.
- Evening: Read, reflect, or brainstorm ideas for the next day.

2. Recognize and Respect Your Limits
Pushing beyond your physical or mental capacity leads to diminishing returns.
How to Respect Your Limits:

- Listen to your body; take breaks when tired or unfocused.
- Avoid overcommitting to projects or unrealistic deadlines.

3. Celebrate Your Wins
Acknowledging your achievements, no matter how small, keeps you motivated and engaged.
Ideas for Celebration:

- Treat yourself to something special after finishing a draft.
- Share your success with supportive friends or writing groups.

Conclusion: Healthy Writer, Creative Mind

Your physical and mental health are the foundation of your creative success. By prioritizing well-being, you not only fuel your creativity but also build a sustainable, fulfilling writing practice. Writing is a marathon, not a sprint, and a healthy mind and body ensure you'll have the energy and passion to enjoy the journey for years to come.

Chapter 23: Designing Your Ideal Writing Life
Building a Sustainable, Joyful, and Productive Lifestyle Around Your Passion

Writing is more than just a profession—it's a way of life. Whether you aspire to be a full-time author or balance writing with other commitments, designing an ideal writing life is about creating a lifestyle that aligns with your goals, nurtures your creativity, and brings you joy. This chapter provides a roadmap to build a sustainable, fulfilling, and productive life centered on your passion for writing.

Why Designing Your Writing Life Matters

1. **Sustainability:** A well-structured writing life prevents burnout and ensures long-term productivity.
2. **Alignment:** Integrating writing into your daily routine helps you stay true to your creative vision and values.
3. **Fulfillment:** Designing a lifestyle you enjoy ensures that writing remains a source of happiness, not stress.

Step 1: Define Your Writing Vision

Before building your ideal writing life, you need clarity about what you want to achieve.

1. Clarify Your Goals

- **Short-Term Goals:** What do you want to accomplish in the next 6 months to a year?
  Examples: Finish a manuscript, publish your first book, or grow your audience.
- **Long-Term Goals:** Where do you see your writing career in 5–10 years?
  Examples: Become a bestselling author, write in multiple genres, or earn a full-time income from writing.

2. Identify Your Values

- What matters most to you as a writer? Creative freedom? Financial success? Connection with readers?
- Let these values guide your decisions and priorities.

Step 2: Create a Writing Schedule That Works for You
A consistent schedule is the backbone of a productive writing life.
1. Assess Your Time

- Track how you currently spend your days to identify available time for writing.
- Use tools like time-blocking to allocate specific periods for focused work.

2. Determine Your Peak Creativity Hours

- Identify when you feel most energized and creative—early mornings, late at night, or somewhere in between.
- Schedule your most important writing tasks during these peak hours.

3. Balance Writing with Other Responsibilities

- If you have a day job, family commitments, or other priorities, find realistic ways to integrate writing.
- Start with smaller time blocks, such as 30 minutes daily, and gradually expand as you build momentum.

4. Experiment with Frequency

- Some writers thrive on daily writing, while others prefer longer, less frequent sessions. Find what works best for you.

Step 3: Build a Supportive Environment
Your physical and emotional environment plays a critical role in your writing success.
1. Optimize Your Workspace

- Dedicate a specific space for writing, free from distractions.
- Equip it with tools and resources that inspire productivity, such as a comfortable chair, good lighting, and a tidy desk.

2. Set Boundaries

- Communicate with family or roommates about your writing time to minimize interruptions.
- Use signals like a closed door, headphones, or a "Do Not Disturb" sign to create focus-friendly zones.

3. Surround Yourself with Positivity

- Decorate your space with items that inspire you, such as motivational quotes, favorite books, or artwork.

Step 4: Prioritize Joy in Your Writing
Writing should be an enjoyable process, not just a means to an end.
1. Reconnect with Your Why

- Reflect on why you started writing and what you love about it.
- Write for yourself first, letting passion fuel your work.

2. Celebrate the Journey

- Acknowledge milestones, no matter how small, such as completing a chapter or receiving positive feedback.
- Treat yourself to something special when you achieve significant goals.

3. Experiment with Playful Writing

- Explore genres, styles, or prompts outside your usual focus to rediscover the joy of creativity.

Step 5: Cultivate Habits That Enhance Creativity and Productivity
1. Start with a Ritual

- Develop a pre-writing routine to signal your brain that it's time to focus.
- Examples: Brew a cup of tea, meditate, or review your outline before starting.

2. Focus on Progress Over Perfection

- Prioritize getting words on the page rather than obsessing over flawless drafts.
- Embrace the messy, iterative nature of writing.

3. Track Your Progress

- Use tools like word count trackers, planners, or apps to monitor your output and celebrate consistency.

Step 6: Balance Work and Rest
Writing is a demanding craft, and balance is essential to sustain energy and creativity.
1. Schedule Rest Days

- Take breaks from writing to recharge and prevent burnout.
- Use this time to engage in hobbies, spend time with loved ones, or simply relax.

2. Incorporate Movement

- Physical activity boosts mental clarity and reduces the strain of long writing sessions.
- Try yoga, walking, or desk stretches to stay energized.

3. Practice Self-Care

- Prioritize sleep, nutrition, and mental well-being to maintain your creative flow.
- Journaling or mindfulness exercises can help process stress and maintain focus.

Step 7: Build a Community of Support
Writing can feel isolating, but connecting with others creates a sense of belonging and motivation.
1. Join Writing Groups

- Participate in local or online writing communities to share experiences and gain feedback.
- Platforms like Scribophile, Reddit's writing communities, or Facebook groups offer opportunities to connect.

2. Find an Accountability Partner

- Partner with another writer to set goals, track progress, and offer encouragement.

3. Engage with Your Audience

- Interact with readers through social media, newsletters, or book signings to stay connected to the impact of your work.

Step 8: Embrace Flexibility
Life is unpredictable, and your writing lifestyle should adapt to changing circumstances.
1. Adjust When Needed

- Revisit your schedule and goals periodically to ensure they still align with your current priorities.
- Be kind to yourself during challenging times, such as illness or personal transitions.

2. Stay Open to Growth

- Experiment with new tools, techniques, or genres to keep your writing life dynamic and fulfilling.
- Seek opportunities for professional development, such as workshops or courses.

Step 9: Plan for Long-Term Success
1. Set Financial Goals

- Create a budget that supports your writing career, including funds for tools, marketing, or conferences.
- Diversify income streams through freelance work, self-publishing, or teaching.

2. Build Your Legacy

- Think about how your work will impact readers and the literary world.
- Consider creating a portfolio that includes books, articles, or other content you're proud of.

Common Pitfalls to Avoid

1. **Overworking:** Writing nonstop can lead to burnout and diminish joy.
2. **Neglecting Health:** Sacrificing sleep, exercise, or nutrition reduces productivity and creativity.
3. **Comparing Yourself to Others:** Focus on your unique journey instead of measuring success against other writers.

Conclusion: Living Your Ideal Writing Life

Designing your ideal writing life is an ongoing process that evolves with your goals and circumstances. By aligning your lifestyle with your passion, prioritizing joy, and fostering balance, you can create a sustainable and fulfilling career as a writer.

Chapter 24: Thriving Through Tough Times
How to Maintain Momentum in Writing and in Life, Even During Personal or Financial Struggles

Life often throws challenges our way—personal loss, financial hardship, health issues, or other crises—that threaten to derail even the most dedicated writers. While these struggles can feel overwhelming, they also present opportunities to cultivate resilience, adaptability, and renewed purpose. Thriving through tough times is not about ignoring difficulties but about finding ways to keep moving forward, both in writing and in life, even when the path seems unclear.

This chapter provides practical strategies for maintaining momentum and staying creative during life's most challenging moments.

Acknowledging the Reality of Tough Times

1. Recognize Your Struggles

- Denying or minimizing difficulties can exacerbate stress. Acknowledge what you're going through without judgment.
- Understand that setbacks are a normal part of life and not a reflection of personal failure.

2. Embrace Imperfection

- During tough times, productivity may fluctuate. Accept that it's okay to work at a slower pace or take breaks as needed.

3. Reframe Challenges as Opportunities

- While hardships are undeniably difficult, they can inspire growth, creativity, and new perspectives.
- Use writing as a tool to process emotions, find meaning, and navigate challenges.

Step 1: Adjusting Expectations
1. Reassess Your Goals

- Temporarily scale down your writing goals to match your current capacity.
  Example: Instead of aiming for 1,000 words a day, commit to 200 or even 50.
- Focus on consistency over output. A small amount of progress is better than none.

2. Prioritize What Matters Most

- Identify essential tasks that align with your long-term vision.
- Let go of less urgent commitments to conserve energy and focus on your priorities.

Step 2: Harnessing Writing as a Source of Strength
1. Write to Process Emotions

- Journaling can help you make sense of complex feelings and gain clarity.
- Use freewriting to explore your thoughts without the pressure of structure or perfection.

2. Channel Experiences Into Creative Work

- Draw on personal struggles to create authentic, relatable stories.
- Writing about challenges can be cathartic and transformative, both for you and your readers.

3. Use Writing as an Escape

- Immerse yourself in storytelling or world-building to find temporary relief from stress.
- Treat writing as a sanctuary—a place where you can focus on creativity instead of problems.

Step 3: Building Resilience and Emotional Strength
1. Cultivate a Positive Mindset

- Focus on what you can control rather than dwelling on circumstances beyond your influence.
- Practice gratitude daily, even for small wins or moments of peace.

2. Develop Healthy Coping Mechanisms

- Engage in activities that calm your mind, such as meditation, deep breathing, or yoga.
- Connect with loved ones for emotional support and perspective.

3. Reframe Failures as Lessons

- Each setback is an opportunity to learn and grow.
- Reflect on what the experience taught you and how it can inform your writing or life decisions.

Step 4: Managing Financial Struggles
1. Diversify Your Income Streams

- Explore freelance writing, editing, or teaching to generate additional income.
- Create digital products, such as eBooks or courses, to tap into passive revenue.

2. Leverage Community Resources

- Seek grants or crowdfunding opportunities specifically for writers.
  Example: Apply for programs offered by organizations like the National Endowment for the Arts.
- Join local writing groups or online communities that provide free resources, advice, or collaboration opportunities.

3. Create a Financial Plan

- Track expenses and prioritize essentials to stretch your resources.
- Use budgeting tools or consult financial advisors to navigate financial challenges effectively.

Step 5: Staying Creative Amidst Adversity
1. Simplify Your Writing Process

- Use tools like voice-to-text apps or notebooks to capture ideas quickly when energy is low.
- Focus on shorter projects, such as essays, poems, or short stories, to maintain momentum.

2. Find Inspiration in Small Moments

- Pay attention to everyday experiences—nature, conversations, or observations—for creative sparks.
- Draw inspiration from the resilience of others or from history, art, or music.

3. Experiment with New Formats or Genres

- Trying something different can reignite your passion and creativity.
  Example: If you're a novelist, write a screenplay or experiment with flash fiction.

Step 6: Building a Support System
1. Connect With Fellow Writers

- Join writing communities, forums, or critique groups to share experiences and gain encouragement.
- Participate in writing challenges or virtual events to stay motivated.

2. Seek Professional Help if Needed

- A therapist or counselor can help you navigate overwhelming emotions or mental health struggles.
- Writing coaches or mentors can provide guidance and accountability to keep you on track.

Step 7: Cultivating Hope and Vision
1. Reflect on Your Why

- Revisit the reasons you write and the impact you hope to make with your work.
- Use your vision to stay focused on the bigger picture, even during setbacks.

2. Celebrate Small Wins

- Acknowledge every step forward, no matter how small.
  Examples: Completing a paragraph, outlining a scene, or brainstorming ideas.

3. Look Toward the Future

- Imagine what success will look and feel like when you overcome your current challenges.
- Use this vision as motivation to keep moving forward, one day at a time.

Examples of Writers Thriving Through Tough Times

1. Maya Angelou

Despite facing significant hardships, Angelou used her writing to explore themes of resilience and hope. Her ability to transform pain into poetry and prose inspired millions.

2. J.K. Rowling

Rowling wrote the first *Harry Potter* book as a struggling single mother on welfare. Her persistence and belief in her story ultimately led to one of the most successful literary franchises in history.

3. Viktor Frankl

During his time in concentration camps, Frankl wrote about the power of finding meaning in suffering, later publishing *Man's Search for Meaning,* a book that has inspired readers worldwide.

Common Pitfalls to Avoid

1. **Pushing Too Hard:** Overworking during tough times can exacerbate stress and lead to burnout.
2. **Isolating Yourself:** Staying connected with others can provide the support and perspective needed to navigate challenges.
3. **Giving Up:** Progress may slow, but perseverance is key to overcoming obstacles.

Conclusion: Writing Through Tough Times

Tough times test your resilience, but they also offer opportunities for growth, self-discovery, and deeper creative expression. By adjusting your expectations, nurturing your well-being, and staying connected to your purpose, you can maintain momentum and emerge stronger, both as a writer and as a person.

Chapter 25: The Infinite Key

Revealing the Ultimate Tool Authors Need: How to Continuously Evolve, Adapt, and Stay Inspired in Any Season, Unlocking Boundless Potential Year After Year

The life of an author is a journey of continuous growth, transformation, and creativity. Success in this field requires more than talent or hard work—it demands adaptability, resilience, and an unyielding connection to inspiration. The "Infinite Key" is a metaphor for the practices, mindsets, and habits that enable writers to unlock their full potential and sustain creativity across the ever-changing seasons of life.

This chapter reveals how to harness this ultimate tool, equipping you to evolve with confidence, adapt to challenges, and maintain a steady flow of inspiration, ensuring that your writing thrives no matter the circumstances.

The Philosophy of the Infinite Key

1. Continuous Evolution

- Growth is not a destination but a journey. Writers must constantly seek new skills, ideas, and experiences to refine their craft.

2. Resilient Adaptation

- The ability to pivot and embrace change is essential for navigating industry shifts, life transitions, and creative blocks.

3. Sustained Inspiration

- True creative potential lies in nurturing an endless source of ideas and motivation, no matter the external environment.

Step 1: Embracing Lifelong Learning

To evolve as an author, commit to constant learning and improvement.

1. Expand Your Knowledge

- Read widely across genres and topics to gain fresh perspectives.
- Take courses or workshops to master new writing techniques.
- Study the works of successful authors to understand their craft.

2. Develop Complementary Skills

- Learn marketing, graphic design, or storytelling techniques to enhance your self-publishing or promotional efforts.
- Explore related art forms, such as filmmaking or photography, to deepen your creative perspective.

3. Analyze and Reflect

- Regularly review your writing to identify strengths and areas for growth.
- Seek feedback from beta readers, editors, or peers to refine your work.

Action Step: Set a goal to learn one new skill or technique each year that enhances your writing journey.

Step 2: Adapting to Change with Resilience

Change is inevitable, but how you respond determines your success.

1. Stay Curious and Open-Minded

- View challenges as opportunities to explore new paths.
- Experiment with different genres, formats, or platforms when faced with roadblocks.

2. Anticipate Industry Shifts

- Stay informed about trends in publishing, marketing, and technology.
- Adapt to new tools, such as AI for editing or social media for promotion, to remain competitive.

3. Build Emotional Resilience

- Practice mindfulness to stay calm and focused during uncertain times.
- Develop a growth mindset, seeing setbacks as steps toward growth.

Example: When eBooks revolutionized the publishing industry, forward-thinking authors embraced the change, leveraging platforms like Amazon Kindle to reach global audiences.

Step 3: Cultivating Endless Inspiration

Inspiration is the fuel that powers creativity. Learn to nurture it consistently.

1. Draw from Life Experiences

- Observe the world around you, paying attention to conversations, behaviors, and emotions.
- Use personal experiences—both joyful and painful—as material for authentic storytelling.

2. Find Inspiration Beyond Writing

- Engage in other creative pursuits, such as painting, music, or theater, to spark new ideas.
- Spend time in nature, museums, or cultural events to stimulate your imagination.

3. Embrace Curiosity

- Ask "what if" questions to explore new story possibilities.
- Dive into topics or historical periods you're unfamiliar with for fresh material.

Action Step: Keep an inspiration journal to capture ideas, snippets of dialogue, or observations that spark your creativity.

Step 4: Building a System for Sustained Growth

1. Create a Personal Development Plan

- Define your short-term and long-term goals for writing and career growth.
- Break these goals into actionable steps and track your progress.

2. Implement Daily Habits

- Dedicate time each day to writing, reading, or skill development.
- Use tools like habit trackers or productivity apps to stay consistent.

3. Schedule Periodic Reviews

- Evaluate your achievements and challenges every quarter.
- Adjust your strategies to align with your evolving priorities and circumstances.

Step 5: Staying Connected to Your "Why"
Your "why" is the core reason you write—it's your source of purpose and motivation.
1. Revisit Your Mission

- Reflect on why you started writing and what impact you hope to make.
- Write a mission statement to remind yourself of your purpose during challenging times.

2. Focus on Your Readers

- Consider how your stories can inspire, entertain, or educate others.
- Engage with your audience to understand what they value in your work.

3. Celebrate Your Progress

- Acknowledge milestones, such as finishing drafts or receiving positive feedback, to stay motivated.

Step 6: Leveraging Community for Inspiration and Growth
No writer thrives in isolation. Building a supportive network is essential.
1. Join Writing Communities

- Participate in local or online groups where you can exchange ideas, resources, and encouragement.

2. Collaborate With Others

- Work on joint projects, such as anthologies or writing workshops, to gain fresh perspectives.

3. Seek Mentorship and Guidance

- Learn from experienced writers or industry professionals who can provide valuable insights.

Step 7: Unlocking Your Infinite Potential

The Infinite Key is not a single tool or technique—it's a mindset and a commitment to continuous growth, adaptability, and passion.

1. Embrace the Process

- Writing is a journey with peaks and valleys. Find joy in the act of creating, regardless of the outcome.

2. Redefine Success

- Measure your success by the fulfillment and growth you experience, not just by external accolades or sales.

3. Leave a Legacy

- Strive to create work that resonates deeply with readers and stands the test of time.

Common Pitfalls to Avoid

1. **Stagnation:** Avoid complacency by seeking new challenges and opportunities for growth.
2. **Overworking:** Burnout stifles creativity. Balance effort with rest and self-care.
3. **Fear of Failure:** Embrace failure as a stepping stone to mastery and success.

Conclusion: The Infinite Key to Your Writing Journey

The Infinite Key is the ultimate tool for unlocking your boundless potential as an author. By committing to lifelong learning, embracing change, and staying inspired, you can evolve continuously, adapt to any season, and create work that resonates deeply with readers. Your writing life is a masterpiece in progress—one that reflects your growth, resilience, and passion.

As you move forward, remember that the key lies within you. Use it to open doors to new opportunities, ideas, and heights of creativity. The possibilities are infinite, and the journey is yours to shape.

Action Step: Take time today to reflect on how you've grown as a writer and identify one new habit or mindset to adopt for unlocking your Infinite Key. Your best work is yet to come.

Message from the Author:

I hope you enjoyed this book, I love astrology and knew there was not a book such as this out on the shelf. I love metaphysical items as well. Please check out my other books:

-Life of Government Benefits
-My life of Hell
-My life with Hydrocephalus
-Red Sky
-World Domination:Woman's rule
-World Domination:Woman's Rule 2: The War
-Life and Banishment of Apophis: book 1
-The Kidney Friendly Diet
-The Ultimate Hemp Cookbook
-Creating a Dispensary(legally)
-Cleanliness throughout life: the importance of showering from childhood to adulthood.
-Strong Roots: The Risks of Overcoddling children
-Hemp Horoscopes: Cosmic Insights and Earthly Healing
- Celestial Hemp Navigating the Zodiac: Through the Green Cosmos
-Astrological Hemp: Aligning The Stars with Earth's Ancient Herb
-The Astrological Guide to Hemp: Stars, Signs, and Sacred Leaves
-Green Growth: Innovative Marketing Strategies for your Hemp Products and Dispensary
-Cosmic Cannabis
-Astrological Munchies
-Henry The Hemp
-Zodiacal Roots: The Astrological Soul Of Hemp
- **Green Constellations: Intersection of Hemp and Zodiac**
-Hemp in The Houses: An astrological Adventure Through The Cannabis Galaxy
-Galactic Ganja Guide
Heavenly Hemp
Zodiac Leaves
Doctor Who Astrology
Cannastrology
Stellar Satvias and Cosmic Indicas
Celestial Cannabis: A Zodiac Journey
AstroHerbology: The Sky and The Soil: Volume 1
AstroHerbology:Celestial Cannabis:Volume 2
Cosmic Cannabis Cultivation
The Starry Guide to Herbal Harmony: Volume 1
The Starry Guide to Herbal Harmony: Cannabis Universe: Volume 2
Yugioh Astrology: Astrological Guide to Deck, Duels and more

Nightmare Mansion: Echoes of The Abyss
Nightmare Mansion 2: Legacy of Shadows
Nightmare Mansion 3: Shadows of the Forgotten
Nightmare Mansion 4: Echoes of the Damned
The Life and Banishment of Apophis: Book 2
Nightmare Mansion: Halls of Despair
<u>Healing with Herb: Cannabis and Hydrocephalus</u>
Planetary Pot: Aligning with Astrological Herbs: Volume 1
Fast Track to Freedom: 30 Days to Financial Independence Using AI, Assets, and Agile Hustles
<u>**Cosmic Hemp Pathways**</u>
How to Become Financially Free in 30 Days: 10,000 Paths to Prosperity
Zodiacal Herbage: Astrological Insights: Volume 1
Nightmare Mansion: Whispers in the Walls
The Daleks Invade Atlantis
Henry the hemp and Hydrocephalus

10X The Kidney Friendly Diet
Cannabis Universe: Adult coloring book
Hemp Astrology: The Healing Power of the Stars
Zodiacal Herbage: Astrological Insights: Cannabis Universe: Volume 2
<u>**Planetary Pot: Aligning with Astrological Herbs: Cannabis Universes: Volume 2**</u>
Doctor Who Meets the Replicators and SG-1: The Ultimate Battle for Survival
Nightmare Mansion: Curse of the Blood Moon
<u>**The Celestial Stoner: A Guide to the Zodiac**</u>
Cosmic Pleasures: Sex Toy Astrology for Every Sign
Hydrocephalus Astrology: Navigating the Stars and Healing Waters
Lapis and the Mischievous Chocolate Bar

Celestial Positions: Sexual Astrology for Every Sign
Apophis's Shadow Work Journal: : A Journey of Self-Discovery and Healing
Kinky Cosmos: Sexual Kink Astrology for Every Sign
Digital Cosmos: The Astrological Digimon Compendium
Stellar Seeds: The Cosmic Guide to Growing with Astrology
Apophis's Daily Gratitude Journal

Cat Astrology: Feline Mysteries of the Cosmos
The Cosmic Kama Sutra: An Astrological Guide to Sexual Positions
Unleash Your Potential: A Guided Journal Powered by AI Insights
Whispers of the Enchanted Grove

Cosmic Pleasures: An Astrological Guide to Sexual Kinks
369, 12 Manifestation Journal
Whisper of the nocturne journal(blank journal for writing or drawing)
The Boogey Book
Locked In Reflection: A Chastity Journey Through Locktober
Generating Wealth Quickly:
How to Generate $100,000 in 24 Hours
Star Magic: Harness the Power of the Universe
The Flatulence Chronicles: A Fart Journal for Self-Discovery
The Doctor and The Death Moth
Seize the Day: A Personal Seizure Tracking Journal
The Ultimate Boogeyman Safari: A Journey into the Boogie World and Beyond

Whispers of Samhain: 1,000 Spells of Love, Luck, and Lunar Magic: Samhain Spell Book
Apophis's guides:
Witch's Spellbook Crafting Guide for Halloween
<u>**Frost & Flame: The Enchanted Yule Grimoire of 1000 Winter Spells**</u>
<u>**The Ultimate Boogey Goo Guide & Spooky Activities for Halloween Fun**</u>

Harmony of the Scales: A Libra's Spellcraft for Balance and Beauty
The Enchanted Advent: 36 Days of Christmas Wonders

Nightmare Mansion: The Labyrinth of Screams
Harvest of Enchantment: 1,000 Spells of Gratitude, Love, and Fortune for Thanksgiving
The Boogey Chronicles: A Journal of Nightly Encounters and Shadowy Secrets
The 12 Days of Financial Freedom: A Step-by-Step Christmas Countdown to Transform Your Finances
Sigil of the Eternal Spiral Blank Journal
A Christmas Feast: Timeless Recipes for Every Meal
Holiday Stress-Free Solutions: A Survival Guide to Thriving During the Festive Season
Yu-Gi-Oh! Holiday Gifting Mastery: The Ultimate Guide for Fans and Newcomers Alike
Holiday Harmony: A Hydrocephalus Survival Guide for the Festive Season
Celestial Craft: The Witch's Almanac for 2025 – A Cosmic Guide to Manifestations, Moons, and Mystical Events
Doctor Who: The Toymaker's Winter Wonderland
Tulsa King Unveiled: A Thrilling Guide to Stallone's Mafia Masterpiece
Pendulum Craft: A Complete Guide to Crafting and Using Personalized Divination Tools
Nightmare Mansion: Santa's Eternal Eve
Starlight Noel: A Cosmic Journey through Christmas Mysteries
The Dark Architect: Unlocking the Blueprint of Existence
Surviving the Embrace: The Ultimate Guide to Encounters with The Hugging Molly
The Enchanted Codex: Secrets of the Craft for Witches, Wiccans, and Pagans
Harvest of Gratitude: A Complete Thanksgiving Guide

Yuletide Essentials: A Complete Guide to an Authentic and Magical Christmas
Celestial Smokes: A Cosmic Guide to Cigars and Astrology
Living in Balance: A Comprehensive Survival Guide to Thriving with Diabetes Insipidus
Cosmic Symbiosis: The Venom Zodiac Chronicles
The Cursed Paw of Ambition
Cosmic Symbiosis: The Astrological Venom Journal
Celestial Wonders Unfold: A Stargazer's Guide to the Cosmos (2024-2029)
The Ultimate Black Friday Prepper's Guide: Mastering Shopping Strategies and Savings
Cosmic Sales: The Astrological Guide to Black Friday Shopping
Legends of the Corn Mother and Other Harvest Myths
Whispers of the Harvest: The Corn Mother's Journal
The Evergreen Spellbook
The Doctor Meets the Boogeyman
The White Witch of Rose Hall's SpellBook
The Gingerbread Golem's Shadow: A Study in Sweet Darkness
The Gingerbread Golem Codex: An Academic Exploration of Sweet Myths
The Gingerbread Golem Grimoire: Sweet Magicks and Spells for the Festive Witch
The Curse of the Gingerbread Golem
10-minute Christmas Crafts for kids
<u>**Christmas Crisis Solutions: The Ultimate Last-Minute Survival Guide**</u>
Gingerbread Golem Recipes: Holiday Treats with a Magical Twist
The Infinite Key: Unlocking Mystical Secrets of the Ages
Enchanted Yule: A Wiccan and Pagan Guide to a Magical and Memorable Season
Dinosaurs of Power: Unlocking Ancient Magick
Astro-Dinos: The Cosmic Guide to Prehistoric Wisdom
Gallifrey's Yule Logs: A Festive Doctor Who Cookbook
The Dino Grimoire: Secrets of Prehistoric Magick
The Gift They Never Knew They Needed
The Gingerbread Golem's Culinary Alchemy: Enchanting Recipes for a Sweetly Dark Feast
A Time Lord Christmas: Holiday Adventures with the Doctor
Krampusproofing Your Home: Defensive Strategies for Yule
Silent Frights: A Collection of Christmas Creepypastas to Chill Your Bones
Santa Raptor's Jolly Carnage: A Dino-Claus Christmas Tale
Prehistoric Palettes: A Dino Wicca Coloring Journey
The Christmas Wishkeeper Chronicles
The Starlight Sleigh: A Holiday Journey
Elf Secrets: The True Magic of the North Pole
Candy Cane Conjurations
Cooking with Kids: Recipes Under 20 Minutes
Doctor Who: The TARDIS Confiscation
The Anxiety First Aid Kit: Quick Tools to Calm Your Mind

Frosty Whispers: A Winter's Tale
If you want solar for your home go here: https://www.harborsolar.live/apophisenterprises/

Get Some Tarot cards: https://www.makeplayingcards.com/sell/apophis-occult-shop

Get some shirts: https://www.bonfire.com/store/apophis-shirt-emporium/

Instagrams:
@apophis_enterprises,
@apophisbookemporium,
@apophisscardshop
Twitter: @apophisenterpr1
Tiktok:@apophisenterprise
Youtube: @sg1fan23477, @FiresideRetreatKingdom
Hive: @sg1fan23477
CheeLee: @SG1fan23477

Podcast: Apophis Chat Zone: https://open.spotify.com/show/5zXbr-CLEV2xzCp8ybrfHsk?si=fb4d4fdbdce44dec

Newsletter: https://apophiss-newsletter-27c897.beehiiv.com/

If you want to support me or see posts of other projects that I have come over to: **buymeacoffee.com/mpetchinskg**

I post there daily several times a day

Get your Dinowicca or Christmas themed digital products, especially Santa Raptor songs and other musics. Here: **https://sg1fan23477.gumroad.com**

Apophis Yuletide Digital has not only digital Christmas items, but it will have all things with Dinowicca as well as other Digital products.